Defining the Word

Understanding the History and Language of the Bible

Defining the Word

Understanding the History and Language of the Bible

John A. Tvedtnes

Covenant Communications, Inc.

CONTENTS

Introduction

We read in the Bible, you recollect, that every man shall be judged according to his works; but it is almost impossible; or, I will say, it is a considerable task and quite a labour to get a community to understand these words as they read; when, in reality, to those that understand them, it is as plain to them as it is for this congregation to count how many fingers I am now holding up before you.

—Brigham Young, *Journal of Discourses* 6:286

Modern readers often find it difficult to read the King James version (KJV) of the Bible. Many of its words no longer mean what they meant four centuries ago. The purpose of this book is to introduce readers to the language of the KJV in a way that will enable them to better understand both the history of the translation and some of the more difficult words and grammatical forms it uses.

The KJV, first printed in 1611, was not translated anew but was based on earlier English translations. That means that its language is even older than the time of King James I, who authorized its publication.

Over the past four centuries, the KJV has been modified, so that our current editions differ in some respects from the first edition, especially in more standardized spelling of words.

This book explores the history of the KJV's English predecessors and the tools available to the early translators. It then
considers the question of scriptural language and examines some
of the KJV printer errors that have occurred from time to time.
(Some of them are quite comical.) Much of the book is designed
to help readers understand the KJV language by describing some
of the major grammatical differences of the text compared to
modern English.

One of the major problems with reading a 400-year-old text
is that the meaning of some of its words has changed over time.
All languages change over time in a process known as linguistic
drift. Each generation uses the vocabulary of its parents in new
ways. The second half of the twentieth century saw words such
as *cool, brother,* and *bad* (to name but a few) redefined by
younger speakers of the English language. If such changes can
take place in a single generation, consider how many more such
changes have occurred since the King James Version (KJV) of
the Bible was first published.[1] The book you hold in your hands
tackles this problem, explaining the older meaning of KJV
words and noting French words that appear in the text.

The latter portion of the book describes spelling variations,
ambiguities, and misunderstandings of original intent in the
KJV. Finally, the appendix consists of the original preface to the
KJV, in which the translators discussed the difficulties of translation and reviewed the work of their predecessors.

Latter-day Saints will find this book especially useful because
the KJV is the official English version of the Bible authorized by
The Church of Jesus Christ of Latter-day Saints. The rationale
for retaining this version is also discussed herein.

NOTES

1 This is one of the reasons the twentieth century saw so many new Bible translations appear in print. Recent years have seen even more updating in the form of the New King James Version of the Bible used by some Protestants.

CHAPTER I

~◞◟~

History of the English Bible

The books of the Old Testament were originally written in Hebrew, though some of them, such as Daniel, are part Aramaic, a language closely related to Hebrew (and employing the same alphabet) that was adopted by Jews living in Babylon and Palestine.[1] As the Jews were scattered to other countries in the eastern Mediterranean basin, it became desirable to make the Old Testament available in Greek, so a translation known as the Septuagint was produced some time between the third and first centuries B.C.[2] Because the New Testament was written in Greek, it became natural for the earliest Christians to use the Septuagint Old Testament, the Greek version most quoted in the New Testament.

Latin became the principal language among literate peoples in the West. In the mid-fourth century A.D., St. Jerome translated the Bible into Latin for use in the western church. Called the Vulgate, from a word meaning "popular" ("for the people"), it was the only authorized Bible in western Europe for many centuries. Indeed, it was not until the early sixteenth century that the Hebrew and Greek Bibles were made readily available in the West, coinciding with the Protestant Reformation.

Anglo-Saxon Translations

In Anglo-Saxon England, the only time people heard the scriptures in their own tongue was when minstrels sang poetic Anglo-Saxon versions of Bible stories. Parts of the Bible, especially the Psalms and the Gospels, were written in Anglo-Saxon during the seventh to ninth centuries. In southern England, around 700 A.D., Aldhelm, Bishop of Sherborne, translated the Psalms into Anglo-Saxon. The Venerable Bede began translating the Bible into Anglo-Saxon and was working on the Gospel of John when he died in 735. Neither Aldhelm's nor Bede's work has survived. Following his coronation in 871, King Alfred the Great authorized translations of the Decalogue (ten commandments), followed by a summary of the Mosaic law, and the letter of the Council of Jerusalem (Acts 15:23–29). These he prefixed to his own law-code. Alfred's court also prepared translations of parts of the Psalms.

A colophon[3] in the Lindisfarne Gospels, prepared ca. 960 by the "unworthy and most miserable priest," the Anglo-Saxon Bishop Aldred, names one Eadfrith as its scribe. The text contains the beginning of Jerome's Preface to the Four Gospels and is a Vulgate manuscript. Aldred's Anglo-Saxon gloss[4] (in the Northumbrian and Mercian dialects) was scratched in between the lines of Eadfrith's script written 260 years earlier. This is the oldest English Bible from the dark ages that has been preserved to our time. It was followed by other Latin Bibles with Anglo-Saxon interlinear[5] glosses. About 990, Aelfric translated the Heptateuch (Genesis through Joshua)[6] with commentaries on the books of Kings and Job and brief versions of Esther, Judith, and Maccabees (the latter two from the Apocrypha).[7]

After the Norman Conquest of England in 1066, parts of the Bible were translated into French for the Norman nobility.[8] During the Conquest, a French version of the Apocalypse was translated into English. It was later used by Wycliffe for his English Bible.

Early English Versions

The superimposition of Norman French on the native Anglo-Saxon language gave rise to the earliest forms of the language we know as English (or Anglish, from Anglo). With the development of written English, clerics and noblemen—and later the masses—became literate.

Richard Rolle (died 1349), the hermit of Hampole, Yorkshire, prepared an English translation from the Latin in the fourteenth century. His text followed the Latin verse by verse. During the same century, an English narrative of the Life of Christ was made up of rearrangements of the Gospels. Another incomplete translation of the Bible was made at about the same time.

In the fourteenth century, John Wycliffe, a theologian at the University of Oxford (later of Lutterworth), supervised the translation of the Latin Vulgate into Middle English.[9] It was the first complete English translation of the Bible. The New Testament, presumably prepared by Wycliffe, was completed about 1380. He used a version of the Apocalypse (Book of Revelation) translated from the French. The Old Testament, completed between 1382 and 1384, was presumably the work of Nicholas Hereford, Wycliffe's colleague.[10] Wycliffe and his associates sought the oldest, most reliable Latin sources before translating. The earliest Wycliffe Bible is a nearly word-for-word translation from the Latin, even employing Latin syntax. About 150 copies have survived to modern times.

Here are the opening lines of Psalms in the Wycliffe[11] and the current KJV versions:

Wycliffe Psalm 22	**KJV Psalm 23**
1 The Lord gouerneth me, and no thing schal faile to me;	1 The LORD is my shepherd; I shall not want.
2 in the place of pasture there he hath set me. He nurschide me on the watir of refreischyng;	2 He maketh me to lie down in green pastures: he leadeth me beside the still waters.

3 he conuertide my soule.
He ledde me forth on
the pathis of riytful-
nesse; for his name.
4 For whi thouy Y schal
go in the myddis of
schadewe of deeth; Y
schal not drede yuels,
for thou art with me.
Thi yerde and thi staf;
tho han coumfortid me.
5 Thou hast maad redi a
boord in my siyt; ayens
hem that troblen me.
Thou hast maad fat
myn heed with oyle;
and my cuppe, `fill-
inge greetli, is ful cleer.
6 And thi merci schal
sue me; in alle the
daies of my lijf. And
that Y dwelle in the
hows of the Lord; in to
the lengthe of daies.

3 He restoreth my soul:
he leadeth me in the
paths of righteousness
for his name's sake.
4 Yea, though I walk
through the valley of
the shadow of death, I
will fear no evil: for
thou art with me; thy
rod and thy staff they
comfort me.
5 Thou preparest a table
before me in the pres-
ence of mine enemies:
thou anointest my
head with oil; my cup
runneth over.

6 Surely goodness and
mercy shall follow me
all the days of my life:
and I will dwell in the
house of the Lord for
ever.

Wycliffe's Bible appeared in various editions to appeal to all classes of people. He sent out groups of disciples, called Lollards, with the Bible and explanation sheets, to read to the people in the streets.

A revision or retranslation of Wycliffe's Bible was issued in 1388, based on better Vulgate manuscripts. It was reputedly the product of one of Wycliffe's students, his secretary John Purvey, assisted at first by Wycliffe himself (who died in 1384), then by some of Wycliffe's associates. Purvey tried to translate the Latin into English sentences, rather than giving a word-for-word rendering. Copies of the Purvey Bible owned by English monarchs Henry VI, Henry VII, Edward VI, and Elizabeth I are still extant. This was the last manuscript (handwritten) English Bible (1395 being the latest copy). Because of the invention of the printing press, all subsequent Bibles were printed.

The movable-type printing press was perfected in 1450 at Mainz by Johann Gutenberg, who produced the first printed Bible (Vulgate version) in 1456. Some forty copies of the Gutenberg Bible are still extant, one in the Library of Congress. It is significant that Gutenberg set up his press in Germany, the country that was to lead the way during the Reformation.

Tyndale's Bible

The Protestant Reformation of the early sixteenth century provided the impetus to make the Bible more widely available. In England, the Reformation met with stiff opposition until Henry VIII's dispute with the Pope. Because popular translations of the Bible were generally seen as attempts to introduce Protestantism, they were discouraged by the English bishops.

Opposition to an English Bible forced William Tyndale, a Cambridge University scholar, to move to Germany in 1524 to continue his translation activities. His initial translation of the New Testament came off the press anonymously at the workshops of Johann Gutenberg's foreman, who had overseen the production of the first printed Bible some years earlier. Tyndale's was the first Protestant translation of the Bible into English and the first printed English Bible.

Tyndale's New Testament met with great opposition from the English bishops. Cuthbert Tunstall, Bishop of London, claimed that he found 3,000 errors in the translation, and Sir Thomas More claimed that many of the errors were willful and designed to promote heresy. The book was solemnly burned at

St. Paul's Cross, London, and the bishops subscribed money to buy up all available copies to destroy them. As a result, of the estimated 18,000 copies printed between 1524 and 1528, only a handful have survived. Ironically, Bishop Tunstall's attempts to buy up all copies of the Bible provided Tyndale with additional funds to continue his work on the Old Testament, while printing more copies of the New Testament and smuggling them into England.

Tyndale was able to publish only portions of the Old Testament before he was arrested and taken to Belgium, where after spending a few months in prison, he was strangled, then burned at the stake on 6 October 1536. Yale University Press reissued Tyndale's New Testament in 1989 and his Old Testament in 1992.

Tyndale's Bible introduced new words and phrases into the English language, including the divine name *Jehovah,* the term *Passover* for the Jewish spring holy day, *scapegoat,* and, more famously, *atonement.* Though the underlying Hebrew word derives from a verb meaning "to cover," Tyndale, wanting to give the idea of a reconciliation with God, invented the term *atonement* in the sense of "union," *at* + *one* + *ment,* with the verbal form atone, "to unite." New phrases introduced into English by Tyndale include "the powers that be" (Romans 13:1), "my brother's keeper" (Genesis 4:9), "the salt of the earth" (Matthew 5:13), and "a law unto themselves" (Romans 2:14).

Coverdale's Bible

While Tyndale was languishing in prison, his assistant, Miles Coverdale, a priest and Austin friar,[12] produced a translation of the whole Bible into English, having it printed at Antwerp and bound in London in 1535. It was a translation mostly from the Hebrew and Greek texts, with heavy reliance on Tyndale's translation, Martin Luther's German version, the Zurich Bible (produced by Swiss reformer Ulrich Zwingli), the Latin Vulgate, the Latin version of Dominican friar Sante Pagninus, plus two other unnamed sources. Coverdale's was the first complete English Bible and was, ironically, dedicated to King Henry VIII, who had condemned Tyndale's work. Coverdale issued a second edition in 1537.

The Bibles of Matthew and Taverner

The first Bible to be printed in England (1537) was Matthew's Bible, prepared by John Rogers, Tyndale's literary executor, who used Tyndale's unpublished translation of Joshua through 2 Chronicles (found in Tyndale's effects when he died the year before), combined with the already-published New Testament, Pentateuch, and Jonah. The rest (Ezra through Malachi) he took from Coverdale, with very slight changes. The book's title page indicates that it was done by license of Henry VIII, and the dedication to the king is signed by the pseudonym Thomas Matthew, to hide Tyndale's involvement. Ironically, this first "authorized" English Bible (i.e., licensed by the government printing authorities) was two-thirds the work of Tyndale, who had suffered martyrdom the preceding year for having translated the scriptures over the objection of the king and clergy.

In 1539, Taverner revised Matthew's Bible to produce a version with better English. Because he was a qualified Greek scholar, he made many more changes in the New Testament. The translation came to be known as Taverner's Bible.

The Great Bible

On 5 September 1538, Henry VIII, at the urging of his queen, Anne Boleyn, ordered that every church should have a Bible translated into English. Thomas Cromwell, who led the Reformation in England, appealed to Coverdale to make a revision, which he based on Matthew's Bible, because much of it was translated from Hebrew and Greek. Coverdale also used Tyndale and his own previous works, referring to the Hebrew, Greek, and Latin. Sebastian Munster compared Coverdale's English text of the Old Testament with the Latin version and suggested changes where necessary. The resultant Bible consequently retained many words and sentences from the Vulgate that were not found in the Hebrew or Greek versions.

The new Bible was published in London in April 1539 and went through seven editions by 1541. Called "Henry's Bible" by some, it was also known as the "Great Bible" because of its large size. The second edition came to be known as "Cranmer's Bible," from Thomas Cranmer, Archbishop of Canterbury, who had written its preface. Cromwell ordered that a copy of the new Bible be placed in each church throughout England, and it became the first Bible authorized for public use.

The Geneva Bible

In 1543 Henry VIII issued a proclamation against the Tyndale Bible and, in 1546 against Coverdale's work. When the king died in 1547, new editions of the Tyndale, Coverdale, Matthew, and Great Bibles were issued. In 1553 Henry's daughter Mary ascended the throne. A devout Catholic, she led a vicious persecution of Protestant leaders, earning her the title "Bloody Mary."[13] Refugees from her purge fled to Geneva, Switzerland, where they found refuge under John Calvin and his successor, Theodore Beza. In 1557 one of Calvin's relatives, William Whittingham, a fellow of All Souls College in Oxford and later dean of Durham, published a small octavo volume of the New Testament. A new Psalter was prepared in 1559. The Psalter and Whittingham's New Testament became the basis for a revised Bible version prepared by Puritan refugees living in Geneva.

The complete Geneva Bible, dedicated to English Protestant Queen Elizabeth I, was published in 1560, with considerable revision to the New Testament. The Great Bible was the basis for its Old Testament, Matthew's Bible for the New Testament. But the committee also used the Latin Bible of Leo Juda (1544) and Pagninus (1527) and consulted the Bibles prepared by Calvin and Beza. The Geneva Bible was the first English version in which the books from Ezra to Malachi had been taken directly from the Hebrew.

The Geneva Bible was the first complete Bible to be divided into verses (following Robert Estienne's Graeco-Latin Bible),[14] to be printed in Roman type, and to use italics for words not found in the original but necessary to the English language. The Apocrypha was included, prefaced by a note concerning its value, but after 1640 it was omitted.

When Elizabeth I became Queen of England in place of her half-sister Mary, she gave permission to have the Geneva Bible published in England, and it ran through 140 editions, seventy of them in Elizabeth's reign alone. Small and convenient, this Bible's portable nature and Roman type made it popular. It was the Bible Shakespeare knew and from which he quoted in his plays. In Elizabeth's day, it was embraced by the Puritans but was not appointed to be read in churches because it was too fundamentalistic. The Geneva version was the Bible carried to America by the Puritan pilgrims. It remained the official Bible in Scotland long after the introduction of the King James Bible, despite the fact that James had been king of Scotland before he also became king of England.

The Bishops' Bible

The Bishops' Bible was commissioned by Matthew Parker, Archbishop of Canterbury, in the time of Elizabeth I and was prepared by a group of sixteen bishops working under him. It was a revision of the Great Bible, without the commentaries and the footnotes. Much of the Geneva Bible was carried into the new work, and it propagated most of the translation and phrasing of Tyndale. The first edition appeared in 1568, the second (with alterations) in 1569, the third in 1572, the last in 1606. Though less popular than the Geneva Bible, it was the official Bible until 1611, when the King James Version was completed.

The Douai Bible

Because the Vulgate was still the official Bible of the Catholic Church, it was inevitable that a new translation from the Latin should appear in English for use by Catholics. Cardinal William Allen, head of the English-language Roman Catholic College at Douai (Douay), Belgium, directed the translation efforts of a group of Catholic exiles from England who had fled when Elizabeth became queen. Though intending to counteract the work of Tyndale and his successors, the group relied on those earlier translations to complete the Douai version. The New Testament appeared in Rheims in 1582, but the Old Testament was not published until 1609–10.

The Douai version was essentially the work of Gregory Martin, formerly a fellow of St John's College, Oxford. The translators had access to a Greek text but rendered mostly from the Latin. Thus, because the injunction "repent" was rendered in Latin *poenitentiam agite,* "do penance," this was the way the Douai version has it. It is widely recognized that the Vulgate Psalms are a great departure from the Hebrew. Jacob Isidor Mombert called the Douai Psalm a "positively unintelligible English version of the unintelligible Latin version of a very uncertain Greek translation."[15] By introducing such a large number of Latin terms to the English language, the Douai sometimes failed in the primary role of a translation—to render the text into a different language. To illustrate, compare the following translations of Numbers 6:17:

Douai	**KJV**
The ram he shal immolate for a pacifique hoste to the Lord, offering withal the baskette of azymes, and the libamentes that by custom are dew.	And he shall offer the ram *for* a sacrifice of peace offerings unto the LORD, with the basket of unleavened bread: the priest shall offer also his meat offering, and his drink offering.

The 1635 Douai edition, published at Rouen, France, had spelling variations but otherwise no noteworthy changes. Because of its many Latinisms and other needs for improvement, it was revised (1749–52) by Bishop Challoner. (In all, the Old Testament went through two revisions, the New Testament five.) Many Latin terms borrowed by the Douai from the Vulgate thereafter became English words. English biblical and ecclesiastical terms that derive from the Vulgate include:

acquisition	election	sacrament
adulterate	elements	salvation
advent	eternity	sanctification
allegory	evangelize	scripture
communion	glory	spirit
congregation	grace	verity
conversion	justification	victim
discipline	penance	
dispensation	propitiation	

In some cases, mistakes made by St. Jerome during his translation of the Bible into Latin were perpetuated in the English, such as his use of "firmament" (denoting something solid) instead of "expanse" in Genesis 1:6–8 (where the atmosphere is meant); and "horns" in place of "rays (of light)" in Exodus

34:29–30, 35, where KJV has "shone." The Douai New Testament of 1582 had an influence on the later King James Version, mostly because of Protestant writings against it.

The King James Bible

Queen Elizabeth died in 1603 and was succeeded by James I, who was then king of Scotland (as James VI). On his trip to London, he was met by Puritans complaining of the excessive "burden of human rites and ceremonies" in the English church. At their request, James called for a clerical conference to be held at Hampton Court Palace in January 1604.

The conference was to discuss "things pretended to be amiss in the Church" by James's Puritan subjects. During this meeting, John Reynolds, president of Corpus Christi College, Oxford, and leader of the moderate Puritan party, expressed the desire to have a more uniform translation of the Bible, acceptable to all parties. Reynolds said of English Bibles, "Those which were allowed in the reignes of Henrie the eighth, and Edward the sixt, were corrupt and not aunswerable to the truth of the Originall." The names of proposed translators were submitted to the king who announced in July 1604 the appointment of fifty-four men to undertake the translation (in the end, only forty-seven did the work).

The translators who worked on the KJV received written instructions thought to have been prepared by Richard Bancroft, who became Archbishop of Canterbury in 1604. An opponent of the Puritans, Bancroft instructed that this version to be undertaken should be an elaborate revision of the Bishops' Bible rather than a new translation, but that the translators were free to make necessary corrections. The same chapter and verse divisions were to be retained.

Because earlier English Bibles sometimes introduced new ideas by means of chapter headings and notes, King James forbade any prefaces or marginal notes except for explanations of Greek and Hebrew words, "having found in them that which are annexed to the Geneva translation, notes partial, untrue, seditions, and savoring too much of dangerous and traitorous concepts. As, for example, Exod. 1:19 where the marginal note alloweth for *disobedience to kings*." The king had also noted many errors of translation in earlier Bibles, and "the worst of all, his majestie thought the Geneva to bee."

After the work of the revision had already begun, the King James translators were given permission to use the Tyndale, Coverdale, and Geneva Bibles to revise the Bishops' Bible, "when they agree better with the text" of the Hebrew and Greek Bible. Familiar passages were to be kept "as they were vulgarly [commonly] used." But from their own accounts, it is clear that they also referred to Spanish, French, and Italian translations; German Bibles by Luther and Zwingli; the Vulgate and other Latin versions; the Syriac New Testament and Aramaic Targum of the Old Testament; and even to the recently published Rheims-Douai Bible of the Catholics.

The committee was divided into six companies, each headed by a clergyman. A group of ten men, headed by the dean of Westminister University, was assigned to translate Genesis through Kings. The second group of eight, headed by the regius professor of Hebrew at Cambridge University, took on the task of Chronicles through the Song of Solomon. The third group, assigned the books of Isaiah through Malachi, consisted of seven scholars under the regius professor of Hebrew at Oxford University. Oxford's regius professor of Greek directed a group of eight in the translation of the Gospels, Acts, and Revelation. All of the New Testament epistles were assigned to seven men led by the dean of Chester and headquartered at Westminster. Finally, a group of seven men at Cambridge, under the direction of the university's regius professor of Greek, translated the books of the Apocrypha.

Each translator worked on chapters or a chapter individually and then met with his colleagues to discuss variations and disputed points. After a company had completed a whole book of the Bible, it was to pass the result to another company, working in the same language, for review. Any questions not resolved between the two companies were then left for a general meeting of the leaders of each company to be held at the end of the proceedings. Other scholars outside the fifty-four were consulted as necessary.

Later, twelve delegates—two from each of the six companies—met daily for nine months at Stationers' Hall, London, as a revision committee. Then there was a full revision by a committee of two, consisting of Dr. Miles Smith (one of the translators) and Thomas Bilson (Bishop of Winchester, appointed from outside the group). Bilson wrote the summaries at the head of each chapter,[16] while Smith is believed to have written the preface, "The Translators to the Readers," which appeared only in the first edition (1611). The full text of the preface appears in the appendix to this guide.

NOTES

1 The term Aramaic derives from the Hebrew name for Syria, *Aram.* In Daniel 2:4, it is called "Syriack," while in 2 Kings 18:26, Ezra 4:7, and Isaiah 36:11, it is termed "Syrian."

2 The term *Septuagint* means "seventy." Traditionally, some 70 or 72 Jewish scholars were involved in the translation.

3 The term *colophon* denotes a note that summarizes a text or describes its history. Usually placed at the end of a passage, it sometimes appeared as a preface. In the KJV, each of Paul's epistles is followed by an English translation of an ancient colophon, in smaller print.

4 The term *gloss* denotes an interlinear or marginal addition to a text.

5 The term *interlinear* means "between the lines."

6 The term *heptateuch* derives from Greek *hepta,* meaning "six." The five books attributed to Moses (Genesis through Deuteronomy) are called the *pentateuch,* from Greek *penta,* "five" (as in *pentagon* and *pentagram*) and in Hebrew are called *Torah,* "law."

7 The Greek Septuagint and Latin Vulgate Bibles included 12 books that were not known from Hebrew versions and that St. Jerome called *Apocrypha* ("hidden"). The books of the Apocrypha were included in early editions of KJV but were later removed.

8 The term *Norman* means "north-man" and denotes the Scandinavian people known as the Norse (cf. the name Norway) or Vikings. These Vikings had conquered the coastal region of France that came to be called Normandy, denoting the origin of its conquerors. The Normans who settled in France adopted the local language.

9 The opening verse (Genesis 1:1) of the Wycliffe Bible illus-

trates one of the problems of translation with theological bias. It reads, "In the first made God of nought heaven and earth." The words "of nought" are not in the Hebrew original. They do, however, reflect the theology of Roman Catholic Europe of the fourteenth century. The synod held at Oxford in 1408 banned study using the Wycliffe Bible.

10 The Old Testament of Wycliffe's first Bible ended at *Baruch* 3:20, with the notation, "Here ends the translation of Nicholas of Hereford." The translator, a Lollard leader, was arrested by authorities who wished to stop his work.

11 In Wycliffe's Bible, it is Psalm 22.

12 The term *friar,* borrowed from French *frère,* "brother," was used of English monks, such as Friar Tuck in the Robin Hood accounts.

13 Mary was the daughter of Henry's first wife, Katharine of Aragon (Spain).

14 Estienne is an early French form of the name Steven/Stephen (modern French uses Étienne). Robert Estienne is often called by the Latin form Stephanus.

15 Jacob Isidor Mombert, *English Versions of the Bible* (New York: A. D. F. Randolph, 1883), 313.

16 In so doing, Bishop Bilson occasionally made mistakes, which were often the result of his theological bias. For example, the heading for Acts 7 speaks of the choice of seven "deacons" for the early Christian church. Since none of the men are termed "deacons" in the text, this was merely a guess based on the kinds of work to which they were assigned, using standards of the Church of England. However, since we later find one of the seven, Philip, preaching, baptizing, and performing miracles (Acts 8:5–13, 26–40) and another, Stephen, seeing the Father and the Son in vision (Acts 7:55–56), it is clear that they were priests or elders, not deacons. The chapter headings for the Latter-day Saint edition of the King James Bible were specially prepared for that edition and are not the ones prepared for the 1611 edition.

CHAPTER II

King James Language

It is a common misconception that the KJV was written in the language spoken in Jacobean England.[1] Actually, it is much older. The Bible authorized by King James and published in 1611 is a revision of the Great Bible then in use throughout England. Written instructions from the Archbishop of Canterbury to the members of the translation committee specified that they were to modify the wording of the Bishops' Bible only when its wording did not agree with the meaning of the Hebrew Old Testament or Greek New Testament texts.

The Bishops' Bible (1569) was itself a revision of the Great Bible (1539), which was a revision of Taverner's Bible (1539), which was a revision of Matthew's Bible (1537), which was a revision of Coverdale's Bible (1535), which was in turn based on the translation made by William Tyndale in 1526–31. Tyndale had relied, in part, on the translation prepared in the late fourteenth century by John Wycliffe and retained some of Wycliffe's wording. Indeed, the King James translators often reverted to Tyndale's wording in preference to that of later Bibles known in their time. A recent study indicates that upwards of eighty percent of the King James Bible comes from Tyndale's verbiage. What this means is that the language of the KJV was already archaic when it was published.

"Scriptural" Language

As the English language evolved, the KJV and other early English translations (the 1582 Douai version for the Catholics and the

1560 Geneva Bible for the Puritans) set the standard for what was considered to be the language of the scriptures. Religious groups like the Quakers tried to keep earlier forms like "thee" and "thou" in their day-to-day speech, often misusing them because the principles guiding their usage were no longer operative.

It is very possible that because the KJV Bible set the standard for scriptural language that Joseph Smith used its style in his translation of the Book of Mormon, the books of Abraham and Moses, and portions of the Doctrine and Covenants. But Joseph Smith was one of many who were brought up with reading the King James Bible and were accustomed to its language.

Nearly a century after the publication of the Book of Mormon, Robert Henry Charles prepared his *magnum opus,*[2] a two-volume translation of ancient texts known as *The Apocrypha and Pseudepigrapha of the Old Testament* (Oxford: Clarendon, 1913). Charles, like Joseph Smith, imitates the style of the King James Bible. He did so because the New Testament cited some of these noncanonical works or earlier writings upon which they depended. Because the KJV was the Bible most commonly read in the English-speaking world, this ensured that readers of Charles's work would more readily make the tie between the various texts. Oxford University Press continues to publish Charles's book. (See the examples in the next section of this chapter.)

Jewish scholar Theodore H. Gaster intermingled KJV language and modern English in *The Dead Sea Scriptures* (New York: Anchor Doubleday, 1956). When citing passages from the Dead Sea Scrolls that were also found in the Bible, he employed the older style of English.

When Robert Lisle Lindsey began his work with the Gospel of Mark in Israel, he initially translated it "into simple modern Hebrew from the Greek text. The text was then distributed to Hebrew-speaking readers and comments invited." Many of those who reviewed the work expressed "the desire that the Gospels, as ancient works, should be read in Old Testament Hebrew style."[3] Lindsey returned to the task and prepared a translation of Mark in biblical Hebrew that has received wide acclaim.

As with Lindsey's modern Hebrew translation of Mark, the Book of Mormon may have been harder for people to accept as scripture had it been in contemporary nineteenth-century English. Americans and Englishmen used to reading the King James Bible may not have seen it as inspired scripture because of the language alone. Perhaps another reason for God's inspiring Joseph Smith to do the translation in the language of the King James Bible was so that it would be easier for readers to recognize when biblical books were being quoted by the Book of Mormon prophets.

Sample King Jamesisms

Here some passages are compared from the pseudepigraphic *Testaments of the Twelve Patriarchs* as translated by Robert Henry Charles in 1913 (using KJV style) and Howard Clark Kee in 1983.[4] Two recent translators, H. W. Hollander and Marinius de Jonge, have, in some cases, preferred to use the KJV style in their 1985 English translation.[5]

Testament of Reuben 5:5
    "*reserved* for eternal punishment" (Charles)
    "destined for eternal punishment" (Kee)
    cf. "*reserved* unto judgment" (2 Peter 2:4; Jude 1:6)

Testament of Reuben 5:6
    "*lusted after*" (Charles, Hollander and de Jonge)
    "filled with desire" (Kee)
    cf. "*lust after*" (1 Corinthians 10:6; Revelation 18:14)

Testament of Simeon 6:5
  "*the Mighty One of* Israel" (Charles, Hollander and de Jonge)
  "the Great One in Israel" (Kee)
  cf. "*the mighty One of* Israel (Isaiah 1:24; 30:29)

Testament of Levi 3:8
  "thrones and *dominions*" (Charles)
  "thrones and authorities" (Kee)
  cf. "thrones, or *dominions*" (Colossians 1:16)

Testament of Levi 8:14
  "*the fashion of* the Gentiles" (Charles, Hollander and de Jonge)
  "the gentile model" (Kee)
  cf. "*the fashion of* this world" (1 Corinthians 7:31)

Testament of Levi 16:4
  "*laid waste*" (Charles)
  "razed to the ground" (Kee)
  in KJV, "*lay/laid waste*" very common; "rase" only in Psalm 137:7

Testament of Judah 16:1
  "*filthy lucre*" (Charles, Hollander and de Jonge)
  "sordid greed" (Kee)
  cf. "*filthy lucre*" (1 Timothy 3:3, 8; Titus 1:7; 1 Peter 5:2)

Testament of Judah 20:3
  "written upon the *hearts* of men" (Charles)
  "written in the affections of man" (Kee)
  cf. "will write it in their *hearts*" (Jeremiah 31:33); "write
  them upon the table of thine *heart*" (Proverbs 3:3)

Testament of Judah 21:5
  "to offer Him the *firstfruits*" (Charles, Hollander and de Jonge)

"to present as offerings" (Kee)
in KJV, *"firstfruits"* very common

Testament of Judah 23:1
"them that have familiar spirits" (Charles)
"ventriloquists" (Kee)
cf. *"them that have familiar spirits"* (Leviticus 19:31; 20:6;
Isaiah 19:3)

Testament of Judah 24:5–6
"And from your root shall rise a *stem*; And from it shall grow
up the rod of righteousness to the Gentiles" (Charles,
Hollander and de Jonge)
"And from your root will arise the Shoot, and through it will
arise the rod of righteousness for the nations" (Kee)
cf. "And there shall come forth a rod out of the *stem* of Jesse,
and a Branch shall grow out of his roots. . . . And in that day
there shall be a root of Jesse, which shall stand for an ensign
of the people; to it shall the Gentiles seek" (Isaiah 11:1, 10)

Testament of Issachar 3:4
"singleness of *eye*" (Charles, Hollander and de Jonge)
"singleness of vision" (Kee)
cf. "thine *eye* is single" (Luke 11:34; Matthew 6:22)

Testament of Issachar 4:1; 7:7
"*singleness* of (your) heart" (Charles, Hollander and de Jonge)
"integrity of heart" [4:1], "sincerity of heart" [7:7] (Kee)
cf. "*singleness* of [your] heart" (Acts 2:46; Ephesians 6:5;
Colossians 3:22)

Testament of Zebulon 7:3
"*bowels* of mercy" (Charles)

"merciful in your inner self" (Kee)
cf. "*bowels* of mercies" (Colossians 3:12)

Testimony of Naphtali 6:7
"we were all scattered unto the *ends of the earth*" (Charles)
"we were all dispersed, even to the outer limits" (Kee)
cf. "the *ends of the earth*" in reference to the scattering (Isaiah
26:15) and gathering (Isaiah 43:6; Micah 5:4) of Israel

Testimony of Gad 4:4
"it *stirreth him up*" (Charles, Hollander and de Jonge)
"he conspires" (Kee)
cf. "*stir him up*" (Numbers 24:9; Job 41:10; Song of
Solomon 2:7; 3:5; 8:4; 2 Peter 1:13)

Testimony of Gad 5:7
"true repentance after a *godly* sort" (Charles, Hollander and
de Jonge)
"for according to God's truth, repentance destroys disobedience" (Kee)
cf. "for *godly* sorrow worketh repentance" (2 Corinthians 7:10)

Testimony of Asher 2:8
"*abstaineth from meats*" (Charles, Hollander and de Jonge)
"is abstemious in his eating" (Kee)
cf. "to *abstain from meats*" (1 Timothy 4:3)

Testimony of Joseph 6:2
"*beguile* me" (Charles)
"lead me astray" (Kee)
cf. "*beguiled* me" (Genesis 3:13; 29:25)

Testimony of Joseph 7:6
"let this *suffice* me" (Charles, Hollander and de Jonge)

"that is enough" (Kee)
cf. "let it *suffice*" (Deuteronomy 3:26; Ezekiel 44:6; 45:9)

An Ancient Practice

Another parallel to this situation is found in the New Testament, where Jesus and his apostles, John the Baptist, and even the angel Gabriel quote passages from the Old Testament. These passages are not rendered into the *koine* Greek, or common, in which the New Testament was written (or, in some cases, perhaps translated) but are taken from the Septuagint Greek translation of the second or third century B.C., which was the Bible of the early Christians. Consequently, they reflect an earlier stage of the Greek language and sometimes do not accurately render the Hebrew original.

Authorized Version

Originally, the KJV was termed the "authorized version" (AV). Today this term still applies to The Church of Jesus Christ of Latter-day Saints, which uses the KJV as its official English Bible. Beginning with the 1979 edition, the Church has provided extensive study tools to its Bible, including revised chapter headings, expanded footnotes, a Bible dictionary, a topical guide, and maps.

Some have questioned the propriety of employing a Bible whose language is no longer current. Perhaps one of the best reasons for retaining the KJV is that we would otherwise lose the close connection between the Bible and other LDS scriptures. Using a modern translation would make it more difficult to see when the Book of Mormon and the Doctrine and Covenants are citing a Bible passage. It would also obscure the correspondence between the Bible and the books of Moses and Abraham in the Pearl of Great Price.

Which Version of the King James Bible?

Many readers assume that the KJV we use today is the same as the original version published in 1611. But they really differ in two respects. The first is that there have been spelling and other minor changes over the last few centuries, in a vain attempt to accommodate the KJV to modern English language usage. Several "revised" versions were produced during the latter part of the nineteenth century and the first half of the twentieth century. While retaining KJV style, the revised versions have corrected some of the mistranslated words in KJV. Some editions of KJV have noted the revisions in marginal notes. There is also a New King James Version that has met mixed reviews.

The second difference involves the books included in the KJV. The original 1611 edition included the twelve books of the Apocrypha, which are known from the Greek Septuagint and Latin Vulgate versions, but not the Hebrew versions of the Old Testament.[6] These are 1 Esdras, 2 Esdras, Tobit, Judith, the Rest of Esther, the Wisdom of Solomon, Ecclesiasticus, Baruch (with the Epistle of Jeremiah), the Song of the Three Holy Children, the History of Susanna, Bel and the Dragon, the Prayer of Manasses, 1 Maccabees, and 2 Maccabees.

The Apocrypha were already questioned by some of the earliest Christian writers in the first centuries following Christ's mortal ministry. Some Protestant Reformers of the sixteenth century removed them from their Bibles, while the Roman Catholic Church affirmed their canonical state in the Council of Trent (1545–63), which was a reaction to the Reformation.

In the 1666 edition of KJV, the Apocrypha was omitted, though many subsequent editions continued to include it. The first official American printing of KJV, in 1782, omitted the Apocrypha, but this did not put an end to the debate. In 1816 the American Bible Society condemned the Apocrypha as "objectionable books." In 1826 the British and Foreign Bible

Society decided to never again include the Apocrypha in its Bibles. Ironically, the only Bibles used at the coronation of British monarchs include the Apocrypha.

The Bible purchased by Joseph Smith and Oliver Cowdery in October 1829 included the Apocrypha. During his revision of the Bible, the prophet Joseph inquired about these books and received the revelation known as D&C 91.

Since 1611, many changes were made to the KJV. Some were deliberate, and a few actually improved the text. Here are just a few examples of changes (in bold) that were later added to the text, along with the year of their introduction.

Matthew 16:16	"Thou art **the** Christ" (1762)
Matthew 26:75	"The word**s** of Jesus" (1762)
Mark 2:4	"for **the** press" (1743)
Luke 1:3	"understanding of **all** things" (1629)

Other changes include the replacement of words. In the following examples, the word in italics (from the 1611 edition) was changed to the one in bold lettering.

Mark 5:6	"he *came*/**ran** and worshipped" (1638)
John 15:20	"The servant is not greater than *the*/**his** Lord" (1762)
Matthew 19:17	"there is *no man*/**none** good but one" (1638)

In 1769 the KJV was revised to modernize its spelling, most of which remains in the current edition.

KJV Printer Errors

Printer errors in various editions have been a constant problem for the KJV; some of them are quite humorous. Because 20,000 copies were required for the first edition of the KJV, there were actually two issues from several presses. A great many discrepancies (most of them minute) were present in the various copies. One of the more important ones, in Ruth 3:15, gave the pair of issues their respective names. In one the text read "he measured six measures of barley, and laid it on her: and hee [Boaz] went into the city." The other read, "and she [Ruth] went into the city." Consequently, the two printings came to be known as the Great Hee Bible and the Great She Bible. Since subsequent editions were prepared from these early printings, the discrepancies were repeated for a time.

The catalog of the British and Foreign Bible Society enumerates nearly 1,000 editions of the KJV between 1611 and 1800. The vast number of typesetting errors that crept into the text during that time is partly due to the fact that the printers bound together sheets from different printings, and the use of these to prepare subsequent printings increased the spawning of errors.

In 1702, Cotton Mather complained of "Scandalous Errors of the Press-work" in which "The Holy Bible itself . . . hath been affronted." He referred to an unidentified edition of the Bible that, at Psalm 119:161, read "Printers have persecuted me" instead of "Princes have persecuted me."

A number of serious errors were committed by Bible printers during the reign of Charles I (reigned 1625–49), son of James I for whom the KJV is named. For example, the Fool Bible inadvertently used the word "a" where "no" was intended in Psalm 14:1, resulting in the reading, "The fool hath said in his heart there is a God." The printers were fined the then enormous sum of £3,000.

The 1631 KJV Bible rendered the seventh commandment, "Thou shalt commit adultery" (Exodus 20:14). This error cost the printers £300 in fines and caused the edition to be called the Wicked Bible or the Adulterer's Bible. Because of the fine, the printing establishment of Barker and Lucas went bankrupt.

The 1638 revision (the first Cambridge edition in folio) read "whom **ye** may appoint over this business" instead of "whom **we** may appoint" in Acts 6:3. Some alleged that Oliver Cromwell had bribed the printers with £1,000 to falsify the text, giving the appearance of biblical support for the appointment of ministers of the church by the people—a notion abhorrent to Anglicans and Scottish Presbyterians but favored by Cromwell's Puritan party.

In the 1653 KJV Bible, 1 Corinthians 6:9 read, "the **un**righteous shall inherit the Kingdom of God," leading to its being called the "Unrighteous Bible." A 1716 printing had Jesus telling a man whom he had healed, "sin **on** more" instead of "sin **no** more" (John 5:14). An Oxford KJV of 1717 had as the heading of the twentieth chapter of Luke, "The Parable of the Vinegar" instead of "Vineyard," and came to be known as the "Vinegar Bible."

An 1801 octavo KJV read in Jude 16, "murderers" instead of "murmurers." An 1804 KJV edition came to be known as the "Murderer's Bible" because in Numbers 35:18, in place of "the murderer shall surely be put to death," it read "the murderer shall surely be put together." An early American KJV published by Jesper Harding at Philadelphia came to be known as the "Dagger Bible" because the typesetter misunderstood the written instructions from the editor and put, instead of the typographic symbol **H,** the word "dagger," by which the symbol is known. In 1 Kings 1:21, this made the text read, "The king shall dagger sleep." A similar error crept into a Cambridge Bible of 1805. The proofreader's marginal instruction "to remain" was incorporated into the text, so that Galatians 4:29 read, "him that was born after the Spirit to remain." This error was repeated in the 1806 and 1819 editions. The accidental inclusion of earlier marginal notes in the Bible text is also known from ancient Hebrew and Greek manuscripts.

In an 1806 KJV edition, the words "the fish**ers** shall stand upon it" (Ezekiel 47:10) were changed to read "the fish**es** shall stand upon it." This error was repeated in 1813 and 1823. The Cockney omission of the initial *h* sound in pronunciation of words may be reflected in the error found in an 1807 Oxford edition at Matthew 13:43, where there is an injunction to him who has "ears to ear." The same edition, in Hebrews 9:14, has "good works" instead of "dead works."

In Luke 14:26 of an 1810 Oxford edition of KJV, the aspirant to discipleship is told to hate "his own wife" instead of "his own life," and it came to be known as the "Wife Hater's Bible." The "Rebekah Bible," printed at London in 1823, says that Rebekah arose with her "camels" rather than her "damsels" (Genesis 24:61). The error undoubtedly arose because the same verse says that "they rode upon the camels" and the word "camels" appears 17 times in that chapter and the singular "camel" once (verse 64).

As late as 1979, in the King James Version printed at Cambridge for The Church of Jesus Christ of Latter-day Saints, the name Joshua is mispelled "Josuha" in Exodus 17:13, though it was corrected in subsequent printings.

NOTES

1   The name James is a distorted rendition of Jacob, hence the historical period covering the reign of King James is termed Jacobean.

2   The Latin term denotes one's "great work," for example, the primary accomplishment of a writer, musician, etc.

3   From Lindsey's introduction to *A Hebrew Translation of the Gospel of Mark* (Jerusalem: Baptist House, n.d.), 76; see also 78–79.

4   See Robert Henry Charles, *The Apocrypha and Pseudepigrapha of the Old Testament in English* (Oxford: Clarendon Press, 1913), 2:282–367, and Howard Clark Kee, "Testaments of the Twelve Patriarchs," in James H. Charlesworth, ed., *The Old Testament Pseudepigrapha* (Garden City, NY: Doubleday, 1983), 1:782–828.

5   H. W. Hollander and Marinius de Jonge, *The Testaments of the Twelve Patriarchs: A Commentary* (Leiden: Brill, 1985).

6   At the time the KJV was translated, the books of the Apocrypha were known only in Greek. Since then, some of them have been found in Hebrew and/or Aramaic versions, including some of the Dead Sea Scrolls.

CHAPTER III

～ ～

Understanding the KJV

To those who might suggest that it is illogical to use a Bible text with language as archaic as the King James Bible, we respond that it is no more illogical than it was for the KJV translators to perpetuate the language of Tyndale and even of Wycliffe in their Bible. The antiquity of the KJV helps remind us that the Bible is, after all, a very ancient text that has been cherished by untold millions over the centuries.

Still, because it was translated nearly four centuries ago, modern readers often have difficulty understanding the KJV. The more practiced readers manage to pick up nuances that the general public would miss, but even they can misunderstand words and phrases that have passed out of usage or have changed in meaning. The purpose of this guide is to help readers understand the KJV as it would have been understood by earlier generations. At the same time, it will promote a better understanding of other scriptures revealed through the Prophet Joseph Smith.

Pronouns

English pronouns can be classified by person and number. Number refers to whether the pronoun is singular (referring to one person) or plural (referring to more than one person). Grammatically, person is represented by first person (the one speaking), second person (the one being spoken to), and third person (the one being spoken of).

Pronouns can also be classified by type or case, such as nominative (used as the subject of a sentence), oblique (used as the direct object of a verb, as the object of a preposition, or as a recipient), and possessive (denoting ownership). From this, we have the following in modern English:

Person	Singular	Plural
First Person		
Nominative	I	we
Oblique	me	us
Possessive	my	our
Second Person		
Nominative/Oblique	you	you
Possessive	your	your
Third Person		
Nominative	he, she	they
Oblique	him, her	them
Possessive	his, hers	their

The pronouns employed in the KJV differ in some respects from this list. For example, while modern English does not distinguish between singular and plural for second person, KJV English has a clear distinction, which can be outlined thus:

Second Person	Singular	Plural
Nominative	thou	ye
Oblique	thee	you
Possessive	thy	your

A further peculiarity of KJV pronouns is that the possessive forms ending in *y* change in form when used before nouns beginning with a vowel and before some words beginning with *h*.

my son	but	*mine* eyes
thy wife	but	*thine* afflictions
my hurt	but	*mine* hand

The form used before vowels is still employed when denoting possession of something unnamed. Thus, while we still say "it is *mine*" but not "it is *thine*," KJV uses both.

Verbal Forms

While verbs tend to be used in modern English in much the same way they are in the KJV Bible, there are some differences of which the reader must be aware. One notes, for example, that past tense often uses the compound form with *did,* while future tense often uses *shall,* rather than the word *will,* which is more common in modern usage. "He did eat" rather than "he ate" (Genesis 3:6).

Modern English adds an *s* to the end of second-person singular, present tense verbs. Thus,

"I come, we come, you come, they come"

BUT

"He come**s,** she come**s,** it come**s**"

In the KJV, in place of *s,* the third-person singular verb form ends in *eth,* as in "he com**eth.**" Verbs ending in a vowel can sometimes take either -*eth* or simply -*th,* giving us "he do**eth**" as well as "he do**th.**" Some of these, however, always take the suffix -*eth*; thus, one can say "she go**eth,** but not "she go**th.**" One of the more common verbs, *to say,* always takes the suffix -*th* "he sai**th.**"

KJV second-person singular verbs are also different from the modern forms in that they end in *st.* A modern speaker says,

"You can do it," where *you* is singular, but the KJV form would be "thou can**st** do it." Some verbs ending in a vowel can take either the suffix -*st* or the suffix -*est,* so that both "thou do**est**" and "thou do**st**" are acceptable. But as with the suffix -*eth/th,* some verbs ending in a vowel must take the longer −*est*: "thou go**est**" is correct, while "thou go**st**" is not. The verb meaning "to say" always takes the form "thou say**est**." Past tense verbs merely add -*st* for second-person singular ("thou said**st** in thine heart"), while future tense uses *shalt,* with the suffix -*t*. The same is true of verbs such as "to have" or "to do" even when used in an auxiliary function. Thus, we have "thou did**st** go" and "thou ha**st** said." (In the latter example, the -*s* at the end of the verb *has* conflates with the -*s* of the suffix -*st*.)

   Imperative or command forms are the same in modern and KJV English, though the KJV often tends to add the pronoun to emphasize whether the original text (Hebrew or Greek) was using singular or plural. This gives us imperative sentences like the singular "Go and do *thou* likewise" (Luke 10:37) and the plural "Receive *ye* the Holy Ghost" (John 20:22), addressed by the risen Christ to his eleven remaining apostles.

Transliteration of Names

Like other translators, the KJV scholars encountered a problem in the transliteration of names found in the Bible. Some of the Old Testament names used Hebrew letters that had no correspondence in English, while Greek names of the New Testament appeared in different forms depending on how they were used in the Greek sentences. To make matters worse, Old Testament names used in the Greek New Testament often differed considerably from their original Hebrew forms.

   Some biblical names had been used in English long enough to have a life of their own, so these forms were retained. For example, the name John was retained in the New Testament, despite the fact that its Greek pronunciation was more like

Yoannes, deriving from the Hebrew *Yohanan* (spelled *Johanan* 27 times in the KJV Old Testament). The apostle named *Yakobos* in the Greek New Testament (from Hebrew *Ya'aqob,* rendered *Jacob* in the KJV Old Testament) was called James, which ultimately derives from the name Jacob.[1]

The English letter *j* originally denoted a *y* sound, as it still does in German. It took on its current sound after the Norman conquest of 1066, when French (with its *zh* pronunciation) was introduced into England. The KJV translators usually opted to transliterate the Hebrew and Greek letters representing *y* by *j*. But there was some inconsistency due to the fact that some 47 different people worked on the KJV translation. Thus, the Hebrew name *Yesha'yah* is variously transliterated Isaiah (most frequently), Jesaiah (1 Chronicles 3:21; Nehemiah 11:7), and Jeshaiah (1 Chronicles 25:3, 15; 26:25; Ezra 8:7, 19). To complicate things still further, the New Testament uses the form Esaias, based on the Greek transliteration of the same name.

Because the New Testament was written (or at least translated) in Greek, which lacks some of the sounds of Hebrew, some Old Testament names have become obscured. The name of the prophet Elijah (Hebrew *Eliyah*) became Elias in the New Testament. As with Isaiah and other Old Testament names, the Greek added a final *s*. Jona in John 1:42 is evidently identical to the name of the Old Testament prophet Jonah, though it is usually rendered *Jonas* in New Testament Greek (Matthew 12:39–41; 16:4; Luke 11:29–30, 32). In John 21:15–17, Peter is called "Simon *son* of Jonas."

Here is a list of some Old Testament persons and places whose names are spelled differently in the New Testament:

Old Testament	**New Testament**
Abijah	Abia
Ahaz	Achaz

Asher	Aser
Beor	Bosor
Boaz	Booz
Canaan	Chanaan
Elisha	Eliseus
Hosea	Osee
Jeconiah	Jachonias
Jehoshaphat	Josaphat
Jeremiah	Jeremias, Jeremy
Josiah	Josias
Jotham	Joatham
Judah	Judas, Juda
Kish	Cis
Korah	Core
Midian	Madian
Manasseh	Manasses
Nahshon	Naason
Naphtali	Nephthalim, Nepthalim
Noah	Noe
Pharez, Perez	Phares
Rahab	Rachab
Rehoboam	Roboam
Sharon	Saron
Shechem	Sychem, Sychar
Sinai	Sina
Sodom	Sodoma
Tamar	Thamar
Uzziah	Ozias
Zadok	Sadoc
Zebulun, Zebulon	Zabulon
Zechariah	Zacharias
Zerah	Zara
Zerubbabel	Zorobabel
Zion	Sion

Because various KJV translators worked on different books of the Bible, the same Hebrew names were spelled differently in different books. For example, note the different spellings in Genesis and Chronicles for the following names, where the translator of 1 Chronicles 1 followed the Hebrew pronunciation more closely than did the translator of Genesis 5.

Genesis 5		**1 Chronicles 1**	
vs. 3	Seth	vs. 1	Sheth
vs. 6	Enos	vs. 1	Enosh
vs. 9	Cainan	vs. 2	Kenan
vs. 15	Jared	vs. 2	Jered
vs. 18	Enoch	vs. 3	Henoch

This pattern is known from other biblical names, both in the listings in 1 Chronicles and elsewhere. For example, the spelling *Absalom* appears 87 times in the KJV, while the more correct *Abishalom* is found only in 1 Kings 15:2, 10. The name of the prophet Samuel (e.g., 1 Samuel 1:20; 1 Chronicles 6:33) is more correctly written *Shemuel* in Numbers 34:20 and 1 Chronicles 6:33; 7:2. The form Samuel is based on the Greek transliteration in the Septuagint Bible. Jacob's second wife is called Rachel in most Bible passages, but the name is spelled *Rahel* in Jeremiah 31:15. The Old Testament name rendered *Simeon* in KJV (Genesis 29:33) appears as *Simon* in the KJV New Testament (Matthew 4:18).[2]

Because the Hebrew letters *aleph* and *ayin* represent sounds with no alphabetic equivalent in English, the KJV translators often represented them by a dot in the middle of the name. Because they have lost meaning for modern readers, these have been removed in the LDS edition of KJV. The translators also employed *ch* to represent two different Hebrew sounds (one of them an aspirated *k*, the other a pharyngeal *h*)[3] that do not exist in English. They borrowed the idea from German words like *ich* and Scottish words like *loch*. The LDS edition of KJV has retained the *ch* but without the underlining.

NOTES

1   Joseph Smith declared, "I have an old edition of the New
    Testament in the Latin, Hebrew, German and Greek
    languages. I have been reading the German, and find it to be
    the most [nearly] correct translation, and to correspond
    nearest to the revelations which God has given to me for the
    last fourteen years. It tells about Jacobus, the son of Zebedee.
    It means Jacob. In the English New Testament it is translated
    James. Now, if Jacob had the keys, you might talk about
    James through all eternity and never get the keys. In the
    21st. of the fourth chapter of Matthew, my old German
    edition gives the word Jacob instead of James" (*History of the
    Church* 6:307).
2   The Hebrew form begins with an *sh* sound, but because this
    sound does not exist in Greek, the New Testament uses an *s*
    sound. The KJV translators opted for an S in place of *sh* for
    this name.
3   Pharyngeal sounds are produced in the pharynx, the upper
    portion of the throat.

CHAPTER IV

～⌒～

KJV Words Whose Meaning Has Changed

All languages change over time, and English is no exception. Some of us remember when *cool* referred to a condition of temperature rather than meaning something akin to "acceptable" and when *bad* really meant "bad." Each generation modifies the language to suit its needs. The result is that when one reads older texts, the meaning can be obscured if we try to read modern meaning into its words.

A few examples will illustrate. In 1838, Joseph Smith wrote that when he told of his first vision, he was persecuted by "professors of religion" (Joseph Smith History 1:22, 75). Modern readers typically think he was writing about people who taught religion in the universities of the time. But in Joseph Smith's day the term often denoted people who *professed* to be religious. For example, in *History of the Church* 5:487 we read, "Early in the morning, Jesse B. Nichols went into the village of Gallsburg, waked up [sic] a blacksmith, and employed him to set a couple of horse-shoes. The blacksmith objected, saying it was Sunday morning, and, being a *professor of religion,* he would not do it unless for double price, which Nichols consented to give him." The blacksmith did not mean that he taught religion, but that he professed to be religious. In a letter of 9 May 1844, D. S. Holister wrote, "On Sunday I was invited to give, in a public discourse, the points of difference between faith of the Latter-day Saints and other *professors* of the Christian religion" (*History of the Church* 6:416–17).

Moving to the KJV, we note that the Hebrew word *nehoshet,* referring to copper and copper alloys, is only once translated *copper* (Ezra 8:27), while the usual term used by the KJV translators was *brass.* In modern parlance, *brass* refers to a copper-zinc alloy that was developed in the sixteenth century A.D., but to earlier generations it referred to any copper alloy. Archaeological discoveries in Israel and in neighboring countries have disclosed that the most common copper alloy in use anciently included tin. It was the Greeks and Romans who first added zinc, lead, and silver to bronze. Consequently, when we read the term *brass* in the KJV, we should generally understand it to mean "bronze," though it may occasionally refer to *copper* alone.

In some passages, the KJV speaks of a "bow of steel" (2 Samuel 22:35; Job 20:24; Psalm 18:34). In each case the Hebrew term rendered "steel" is *nehoshet,* which, as has already been noted, really refers to copper and copper alloys. The same word is also rendered "steel" in Jeremiah 15:12. Clearly, the KJV word does not refer to the iron-carbon alloy that we call "steel" in our day. Rather, it refers to something that is hard, a meaning reflected in our verb "to steel," which means "to harden." In both KJV English and in the English of Joseph Smith's day, the noun "steel" could refer to any hard metal.

The following words found in the KJV Bible are often confusing to readers because they are understood differently in our time or have fallen into disuse. Some of them were French words introduced into English during the Norman conquest of England in 1066 by William the Conqueror, and sometimes discontinued in English.[1] The scriptural references do not always list all occurrences of the word in the KJV, nor is the KJV text always an accurate rendition of the underlying Hebrew and Greek text.

abase *put down, lower* (Job 40:11; Isaiah 31:4; Ezekiel 21:26; Daniel 4:37; Matthew 23:12), a French borrowing

abide (past tense: **abode**), *stay, remain* (John 11:6, where JST uses "tarry," described below)

above sometimes means *more than* (Genesis 3:14; 48:22; 49:26; Exodus 19:5; Deuteronomy 7:6, 14; 14:2; Judges 5:24; 1 Kings 16:30; Luke 13:2, 4)

addict *devote oneself* (1 Corinthians 16:15)

adventure *risk* (Deuteronomy 28:56; Judges 9:17; Acts 19:31); cf. *venture,* "try"

advertise *notify, inform* (Numbers 24:14; Ruth 4:4)

afore *before, earlier* (2 Kings 20:4; Psalm 129:6; Isaiah 18:5; Ezekiel 33:22; Romans 1:2; 9:23; Ephesians 3:3)

aforehand *beforehand, in advance* (Mark 14:8)

aforetime *formerly, previously, anciently* (Nehemiah 13:5; Job 17:6; Isaiah 52:4; Jeremiah 30:20; Daniel 6:10; John 9:13; Romans 15:4)

albeit *though, although* (Ezekiel 13:7; Philemon 1:19)

allow sometimes means *acknowledge* (Luke 11:48; Acts 24:15)

ambassage *embassy, delegation* (Luke 14:32), a French borrowing

amend sometimes means *repair* (2 Chronicles 34:10). Note the meaning of "mend" and its relationship to KJV idioms such as "**amend** one's ways" (Jeremiah 7:3, 5; 26:13; 35:15). For **amend** in the sense of being healed (i.e., mended), see John 4:52.

amerce *levy a fine* (Deuteronomy 22:19)

anon *soon* (Matthew 13:20; Mark 1:30)

approve sometimes means *prove* (Philippians 1:10; 2 Corinthians 7:11)

assay *try* (Acts 9:26; Job 4:2); cf. French *essayer,* "try, attempt"

attain sometimes means *arrive* (Acts 27:12)

attend sometimes means *serve, wait upon* (Esther 4:5; Romans 13:6; 1 Corinthians 7:35; Hebrews 7:13); cf. French *attendre,* "wait." In some cases, it means *listen, hear* (Psalms 17:1; 55:2; 61:1; 66:19; 86:6; 142:6; Proverbs 4:1, 20; 5:1; 7:24; Acts 16:14); cf. French *entendre,* "listen."

beeves *bovines,* i.e., cows and bulls (Leviticus 22:19, 21; Numbers 31:28, 30, 33, 38, 44); from French *boeuf,* "ox," origin of English "beef"[2]

beguile sometimes means *cheat* (Genesis 29:25; Colossians 2:18)

behove *behoove* (Luke 24:46; Hebrews 2:17)

beset *surround, besiege* (Judges 19:22; 20:5; Psalms 22:12; 139:5; Hosea 7:2; Hebrews 12:1)

besom *broom,* name of a plant used for sweeping (Isaiah 14:23)

besought *looked for, asked for, entreated, requested* (Genesis 42:21; Exodus 32:11; Deuteronomy 3:23; 2 Samuel 12:16; Matthew 8:31, 34; John 19:38; Acts 21:12)

bestead *profited, accommodated* (Isaiah 8:21)

bestir (oneself) *rouse to action* (2 Samuel 5:24; cf. Alma 60:29)

betimes *early* (Genesis 26:31; 2 Chronicles 36:15; Job 8:5; 24:5; Proverbs 13:24). Compare the Chronicles passage with the use of "early" in KJV of Jeremiah 7:13, 25; 11:7; 25:3–4; 26:5; 29:19; 32:33; 35:14–15; 44:4.

bolled *in bloom* (Exodus 9:31); cf. boll weavel, an insect that infects cotton plants

bond sometimes means *slave* (1 Corinthians 12:13; Galatians 3:28; Ephesians 6:8; Colossians 3:11; Revelation 13:16; 19:18; cf. 2 Nephi 10:16; 26:33; Alma 1:30; 5:49; 11:44; 4 Nephi 1:3; D&C 43:20)

botch *swollen sore,* like a boil (Deuteronomy 28:27, 35); cf. blotch

bottle *wineskin,* a leather container (Genesis 21:14–15, 19; Joshua 9:4, 13; Job 32:19; Matthew 9:17). The pottery bottle of Jeremiah 19:1 is really a flask and employs a different Hebrew word.

brigandine *armor* (Jeremiah 51:3)

brimstone *sulfur/sulphur* (Genesis 19:24; Deuteronomy 29:23; Psalm 11:6; Revelation 9:17–18; 14:10; 19:20; 20:10; 21:8). The KJV word derives from *brunston,* "burning stone."

bruit *noise, rumor* (Jeremiah 10:22; Nahum 3:19). *Bruit* in Jeremiah 10:22 means "report." The French word means "noise," but in slang it became "rumor," whence the KJV usage. This makes the passage redundant: "Behold, the **noise** of the **bruit** is come."

bulrush *reed* (Exodus 2:3; Isaiah 18:2; 58:5). The Hebrew text of the first two references employs the Egyptian word for *papyrus plant,* found also in Job 8:11 (paralleling *flag,* discussed below) and Isaiah 35:7, where KJV translate it **rush.**

careful When Paul wrote "Be careful for nothing" (Philippians 4:6), he did not mean that caution should not be exercised; rather, he was admonishing his reader not to be *concerned, worried, or anxious,* i.e., to have no cares (see also Jeremiah 17:8).

carriage does not imply travel in wagons. It means "that which is carried," i.e., *luggage, baggage* (1 Samuel 17:22; Isaiah 46:1; Acts 21:15).

casement *window* (Proverbs 7:6)

cattle usually denotes herd animals, including bovines (cows) and (more often) sheep and goats (Genesis 4:20; 29:7; 30:32) but sometimes refers to mammals in general (Genesis 1:24–26; 6:20; 7:14). The English derives from an older term meaning "wealth, possessions," and the same is true of the Hebrew *miqneh,* one of several Hebrew terms rendered "cattle" in KJV (e.g., Genesis 13:2).

cause as a noun means *reason* (1 Samuel 17:29; 19:5; Job 2:3; Matthew 5:22; John 12:27)

chambering *illicit sexual relations* (Romans 13:13)

chapman *traveling merchant, peddler* (2 Chronicles 9:14)

charger *platter* (Numbers 7:13; Matthew 14:8)

chide (past tense: **chode**) *argue, dispute, find fault* (Genesis 31:36; Exodus 17:2; Numbers 20:3; Judges 8:1; Psalm 103:9)

choler *anger* (Daniel 8:7; 11:11); cf. French *colère,* "anger"

ciel *cover, overlay,* from French *ciel,* "sky" (2 Chronicles 3:5); cf. *ceiling* (1 Kings 6:15)

closet means *closed place,* so when Jesus admonished his disciples to "enter into thy *closet,* and when thou hast shut thy door, pray to thy Father" (Matthew 6:6), he meant that they should offer personal prayers in places where no one would see or hear them. Modern closets, places where one hangs clothes, did not exist in Christ's time nor in the time of the KJV. Even today, many people in Europe and elsewhere put their clothing into wooden armoires, not in small rooms such as those so widely used in the U.S. The word *closet* in Joel 2:16 refers to a place where the bride was concealed until time to deliver her to her new husband. The practice continues to this day in some parts of the world.

coast means *border,* not "seashore" (e.g., Deuteronomy 16:4; 19:8; Judges 19:29; 1 Samuel 11:3, 7; 1 Kings 1:3; 1 Chronicles 4:10; 2 Chronicles 11:13; Matthew 19:1; Acts 26:20). In some cases, it is used in reference to areas far from the sea (e.g., Judges 1:36; 11:20, 22, 26; 1 Samuel 6:9; 2 Kings 15:16; Matthew 2:16; 16:13; 19:1; Mark 7:31; 10:1).

commit . . . unto The verb in the Greek version of John 2:24 means *trust.* In KJV, John 2:24–25 reads "But Jesus did not *commit himself unto* them, because he knew all men [a single word meaning "everyone"], And needed not that any should testify of man: for he knew what was in man" (italics added). In this case, it means that Jesus did not trust the people with his divine identity. In modern colloquial English, we might say that "Jesus did not give himself away" as the Son of God.

communicate sometimes means *share* (Philippians 4:14; 1 Timothy 6:18; Hebrews 13:16)

company In KJV English, this term can be either a noun or a verb. As a verb, it means *associate, accompany,* or *keep company with* (Acts 1:21). As a noun, it denotes a *group*. For an example of its use as a noun meaning *companions* or *associates,* see Numbers 16:5–6.

compass as a noun means *circumference, edge, rim* (Exodus 27:5; 38:4; 1 Kings 7:23, 35). The magnetic compass was so named because of its round shape and the round appearance of the horizon when determining direction. The instrument known as the Liahona, which the Lord prepared for Lehi, is usually called a "compass" because of its shape (1 Nephi 16:10, 16, 26–30; 18:12, 21; 2 Nephi 5:12; Alma 37:38, 43–44). It was not a magnetic compass, for the spindles pointed the direction Lehi's party should travel, not a magnetic compass direction such as north.

compass as a verb means *surround, go around, encircle,* as does "fetch a compass" (Numbers 21:4; 34:5; Joshua 6:3–4, 7; 15:3; 1 Kings 7:15; 2 Kings 11:8; Job 16:13; 40:22; Luke 19:43) or, in military terms, *outflank* (2 Samuel 5:23)

considered *understood* (Mark 6:52)

contemn *despise* (Psalms 10:13; 15:4; 107:11)

convenient sometimes means *suitable* (Proverbs 30:8; Mark 6:21; Ephesians 5:4)

conversation *conduct, behavior* (Psalms 37:14; 50:23; 2 Corinthians 1:12; Galatians 1:13; Ephesians 2:3; 4:22; Philippians 1:27; 3:20; 1 Timothy 4:12; Hebrews 13:5, 7; James 3:13; 1 Peter 1:15, 18; 2:12; 3:1–2, 16; 2 Peter 2:7; 3:11)

corn *grain,* not *maize* (see especially John 12:24, where we have "a corn of wheat")

couch sometimes means *crouch, lie down* (Genesis 49:9, 14; Numbers 24:9; Job 38:40)

countervail *counteract* (Esther 7:4)

covert is used as an adjective in modern English in the meaning "hidden," but KJV employs it as a noun meaning *hiding place* (1 Samuel 25:20; 2 Kings 16:18; Job 38:40;[3] 40:21; Psalm 61:4; Isaiah 4:6; 16:4; 32:2; Jeremiah 25:38). The term is related to **cover,** from French *couvrir.*

cruse *jug, jar, bottle* (1 Samuel 26:11–12, 16; 1 Kings 14:3; 17:12, 14, 16; 19:6; 2 Kings 2:20)

curious *skilled, skillfully wrought,* not *strange* or *inquisitive* (Exodus 35:32; Psalm 139:15). It had the same meaning in Joseph Smith's day (in the Book of Mormon, see "The Testimony of Eight Witnesses"; 1 Nephi 16:10; 18:1; Alma 37:39; 63:5; Helaman 6:11; Ether 10:27).

damnation *judgment* (Matthew 23:14, 33; Mark 3:29; 12:40; Luke 20:47; John 5:29; Romans 3:8; 13:2; 1 Corinthians 11:29; 1 Timothy 5:12)

damsel *girl,* literally *small woman*[4] (Genesis 24:14, 16, 28, 55, 57; 34:3–4; Mark 5:39–41). In the account that parallels the

Mark passage, Luke 8:51, 54, the girl is called *maiden* and *maid* by KJV, a term discussed below.

daysman *arbitrator* (Job 9:33)

dayspring *dawn, daybreak* (Job 38:12; Luke 1:78)

degrees in the Psalms denotes a *staircase* on which the Levites would sing in the temple (see the first verse of each of Psalms 120–134)

desert place is not a sandy wasteland, but rather a place where no one dwells, i.e., a *deserted place* (Exodus 3:1; Matthew 14:13, 15; Mark 1:45; 6:31–32, 35; Luke 4:42; 9:10, 12)

dirt in one instance translates from the Hebrew word meaning *excrement* (Judges 3:22)

discover usually means *uncover, reveal* rather than "find" (Deuteronomy 22:30; 1 Samuel 14:8; Proverbs 25:9; Isaiah 3:17; Ezekiel 16:37)

draw sometimes means *pull* (Psalm 10:9; Isaiah 5:18; John 21:6)

ear (the ground) *work* or *plow* (1 Samuel 8:12; Isaiah 30:24)

earth in KJV is not the planet. The Hebrew word *'erets* is most often rendered "land" (e.g., Genesis 47:27). Thus, when Balak complained of Israel that "there is a people come out from Egypt: behold, they cover the face of the earth" (Numbers 22:5), he could not have meant that they covered the entire planet.

emerods *hemorrhoids* (Deuteronomy 28:27; 1 Samuel 5:6, 9, 12; 6:4–5, 11, 17), though the Hebrew term meant something else, perhaps bubonic plague

ensue *pursue* (1 Peter 3:11)

environ *encircle,* from French *environ,* "surrounding" (Joshua 7:9); cf. English "environment"

epistle *letter.* Contrary to what some may think, the term does not mean "sacred letter" but denotes any and all letters.

eschew *shun, avoid* (Job 1:1, 8; 2:3; 1 Peter 3:11)

establish sometimes means *affirm,* in the sense of *make firm or stable* (Numbers 30:13–14; Deuteronomy 19:15; Romans 1:11; 3:31; 10:3)

evil has taken on a special meaning in modern English, in that it generally refers to sin committed against God and humanity. The KJV term, however, merely means *bad.* Hence, in Jeremiah 24:3, the *evil* figs were "bad" rather than "sinful."

fain *gladly* (Job 27:22; Luke 15:16; cf. Alma 12:14; Abraham 1:27)

faint means *be discouraged* or *lose confidence,* not *pass out, become unconscious* (Luke 18:1)

feller In Isaiah 14:8, the trees rejoice that "no **feller** is come up against us." Some modern Bible readers understand this to be "fellow," but it actually refers to one who "fells" trees.

fenced cities *walled cities* (e.g., Numbers 32:17, 36)

fillet *thread, cord,* from French *fille* (Exodus 27:10; Jeremiah 52:21)

flag *reed* (Exodus 2:3, 5; Job 8:11; Isaiah 19:6)

foot sometimes means *base* or *bottom,* as in English "foot of the mountain" (Exodus 30:18, 28; 31:9)

fray *frighten, scare* (Deuteronomy 28:26; Jeremiah 7:33; Zechariah 1:21); cf. *afraid*

froward *disobedient* (Deuteronomy 32:20; 2 Samuel 22:27; Job 5:13; Psalms 18:26; 101:4; Proverbs 2:12, 15; 3:32; 1 Peter 2:18)

fuller *laundryman* (Mark 9:3)

furniture *furnishings, accouterments, supplies,* i.e., that which is furnished (Genesis 31:34; Exodus 31:7–9; 35:14; 39:33; Nahum 2:9)

gainsay *contradict* (Luke 21:15; Acts 10:29)

gall is thought by some scholars to be the juice of the opium poppy (Matthew 27:34)

garner *grain silo* (Psalm 144:13; Joel 1:17; Matthew 3:12; Luke 3:17; cf. Alma 26:5; D&C 101:65)

gat past tense of *got,* most often used in KJV in reference to the motion of human beings (Genesis 19:27; Exodus 24:18; Numbers 11:30; 14:40; 16:27; Judges 9:48, 51; 19:28; 1 Samuel 13:15; 24:22; 26:12; 2 Samuel 4:7; 13:29; 17:23; 19:3)

gay *fine, rich* (of clothing in James 2:3)

ghost *spirit.* Because English is a Germanic language with an overlay of French, it has both *ghost* (cf. German *geist*) and *spirit* (from French *esprit*). In the KJV, both mean the same thing.

Hence, we have both Holy Ghost (Acts 8:19) and Holy Spirit (Luke 11:13), from the same Greek expression.

gin *snare, trap;* in Job 18:8–9 it is listed with "net" and "snare," while in Isaiah 8:14 and Amos 3:5 it parallels "snare"[5]

glass *mirror* (1 Corinthians 13:12; 2 Corinthians 3:18; James 1:23); called a "looking glass" in Job 37:18. The earliest mirrors were not made of the material we call "glass" but of polished metal.[6]

goodman *master, owner* (Proverbs 7:19; Matthew 20:11; 24:43; Mark 14:14; Luke 12:39; 22:11)

governor in James 3:4 denotes the *rudder* of a ship

grisled *grizzled, streaked* or *sprinkled with gray,* from French *gris,* "gray" (Genesis 31:10, 12; Zechariah 6:3, 6)

gutter *watercourse* (Genesis 30:38, 41; 2 Samuel 5:8)

hale *drag* (Luke 12:58)

halt as a verb, it literally meant *limp,* not *hesitate* or *stop* (1 Kings 18:21). The noun form means "lame" (Matthew 18:8; Mark 9:45; Luke 14:21; John 5:3).

hap *luck, lot* (Ruth 2:3)

haply *by chance, by luck* (as in *perhaps* or the older *mayhap*), not *happily* (1 Samuel 14:30; 2 Corinthians 9:4)

hard followed by a preposition (by, unto, upon, after) means *near, close, next to, adjacent to* (Leviticus 3:9; Judges 9:52; 20:45;

1 Samuel 14:22; 31:2; 2 Samuel 1:6; 1 Kings 21:1; 1 Chronicles 10:2; 19:4; Psalms 63:8; 88:7; Acts 18:7)

hardly sometimes means *harshly* (Genesis 16:6), sometimes *with difficulty* (Matthew 19:23; Luke 9:39; Acts 27:8)

haunt (place) *frequent, usual* (1 Samuel 23:22; 30:31; Ezekiel 26:17)[7]

hold *stronghold, fortress* (1 Samuel 22:4-5; 2 Samuel 5:17; 23:14); cf. **strong hold** in 2 Samuel 5:7; 24:7.[8] The same Hebrew word is rendered "castle" in the parallel account in 1 Chronicles 11:5, 7.

holden *held* (2 Kings 23:22–23; Job 36:8; Psalms 18:35; 71:6; 71:23; Acts 2:24)

holpen *helped,* from an old Germanic form (Psalms 83:8; 86:17; Isaiah 31:3; Daniel 11:34; Luke 1:54)

hosen is the Germanic plural of *hose* (as in stockings), perhaps referring to a garment like trousers or breeches, though some think it is a tunic (Daniel 3:21)

hough *hamstring* (Joshua 11:6, 9; 2 Samuel 8:4)

howbeit *however* (Judges 4:17; Ruth 3:12; 2 Samuel 2:23; Matthew 17:21)

husbandman *gardener, farmer* (Genesis 9:20; 2 Kings 25:12; John 15:1; 2 Timothy 2:6)

ill favoured *ugly* (Genesis 41:3–4, 19–21, 27)

impute is related to "compute," sometimes meaning *to account* or *to count* (Leviticus 7:18; Romans 4:6, 8, 22, 24; 5:13; 2 Corinthians 5:19)

instant *urgent* (Luke 23:23; 2 Timothy 4:2); **instantly** *urgently* (Luke 7:4)

jeopardy (verb) *risk, imperil, endanger* (Judges 5:18), whence the noun **jeopardy** (2 Samuel 23:17; 1 Chronicles 11:19; 12:19; Luke 8:23; 1 Corinthians 15:30)

kine *bovines,* i.e., cows and bulls (Genesis 32:15; 41:2–4, 18–20, 26–27; Deuteronomy 7:13; 28:4, 18, 51; 32:14; 1 Samuel 6:7, 10, 12, 14; Amos 4:1)

laver *washing basin,* from French *laver,* "to wash" (Exodus 30:18, 28)

leasing (noun) *lie, falsehood* (Psalms 4:2; 5:6)

leave as a noun means *permission* (Numbers 22:13; Mark 5:13; John 19:38)

leave off *cease, stop, end* (Genesis 11:8; 17:22; 1 Kings 15:21; Job 32:15; Jeremiah 38:27; Nehemiah 5:10; Proverbs 17:14)

lien *lain* (Genesis 26:10; Psalm 68:13; Jeremiah 3:2)

let means *hinder, prevent,* not *permit* (Romans 1:13; 2 Thessalonians 2:7)

liken *compare* (Psalm 89:6; Isaiah 40:18, 25; 46:5; Jeremiah 6:2; Matthew 7:24, 26)

likeness (noun) *form, shape* (Genesis 1:26; 5:1, 3; Exodus 20:4; Deuteronomy 4:16–18)

liquor any *liquid* (Exodus 22:29). In Numbers 6:3 and Song of Solomon 7:2, it refers to an alcoholic beverage.

list *want, desire, wish* (Matthew 17:12; John 3:8; James 3:4; cf. Mosiah 2:32–33, 37; Alma 3:26–27; 26:6)

lively sometimes means *living, alive* (Acts 7:38; 1 Peter 1:3; 2:5)

loins *lower portion of back,* often used euphemistically to denote the sex organs (Genesis 35:11; 37:34; 46:26; Exodus 1:5; 1 Kings 12:10; 18:46; 20:31–32)

lucre *gain* (1 Samuel 8:3; 1 Timothy 3:3, 8; Titus 1:7, 11; 1 Peter 5:2)

magnifical *magnificent* (1 Chronicles 22:5)

maid, maiden can denote a *female slave* (Genesis 16:2–3, 5–6, 8; 30:18; Leviticus 25:6; Isaiah 24:2; Psalm 123:2) or a *virgin* (Exodus 22:16; Deuteronomy 22:14, 17; Judges 19:24). In Leviticus 12:5, it means *female.*

make an end *finish* (Genesis 27:30; 49:33; Exodus 31:18; Deuteronomy 31:24; 32:45). The idiom is common in the Book of Mormon.

malefactor *evildoer;* cf. French *mal,* "bad," and *faire* (older *facter*), "do" (Luke 23:32, 39; John 18:30)

manger *feeding trough,* from French *manger,* "to eat" (Luke 2:7)

marishes *marshes* (Ezekiel 47:11)

master can mean *owner* (e.g., of a slave), but sometimes means *teacher* (Matthew 8:19; Mark 9:38; 10:35; Luke 9:49; John 1:38)

meat means *food* (that which is **eat**en), not animal flesh (Genesis 1:29–30; Isaiah 62:8; John 4:8). Hence, when the resurrected Jesus asked for "meat," he was given fish and a honeycomb (Luke 24:41–43).

meet usually has the same meaning as in modern English, but sometimes means *equal to, equivalent to, matching, corresponding to* (Genesis 2:18, 20), *suitable* (Deuteronomy 3:18; Esther 2:9; Ezekiel 15:4–5; 1 Corinthians 15:9), *expedient, desirable, proper, fit* (Exodus 8:26; Ezra 4:14; Job 34:31; Jeremiah 26:14; 27:5; Matthew 15:26; Luke 15:32), *necessary* (Proverbs 11:24; Matthew 3:8; Acts 26:20)

mete *measure* (Exodus 16:18; Matthew 7:2; Mark 4:24; Luke 6:38); cf. the modern term *meter* and see **meteyard** in Leviticus 19:35

mischief sometimes means *misfortune* (Genesis 42:4, 38; 44:29; Exodus 21:22–23; 2 Kings 7:9; Proverbs 17:20)

mote *straw* (Matthew 7:3–5)

nail *tent peg* (Judges 4:21–22; 5:26; Ezra 9:8; Isaiah 22:23, 25)

nether *lower* (Exodus 19:17; Deuteronomy 24:6; Joshua 15:19; Judges 1:15; Job 41:24; Ezekiel 31:14, 16, 18)

nigh *near* (Genesis 47:29; Exodus 24:2; John 19:42)

occupy sometimes means *use* (Exodus 38:24; Judges 16:11); cf. *occupied* for restrooms

or ever *before* (Psalm 90:2; Proverbs 8:23; Daniel 6:24; Acts 23:15)

ordain *appoint, proclaim, declare, decree* (Numbers 28:6; 1 Kings 12:32–33; 1 Chronicles 9:22; 17:9; Isaiah 26:12; 1 Corinthians 7:17; Titus 1:5). In modern times, we generally think of this term as denoting a formal ceremony whereby someone receives priesthood, but this is a narrower meaning than that used in KJV.

ordinance is the noun form of **ordain** and denotes *something appointed, proclaimed,* or *decreed* (Exodus 12:43; 13:10; 15:25; 18:20; Leviticus 18:3–4; 1 Corinthians 11:2; Ephesians 2:15; 1 Peter 2:13). In KJV it does not necessarily denote a formal religious rite.

organ denotes any instrument, but especially wind instruments, though in the Bible it translates the Hebrew word for *lute* or *flute* (Genesis 4:21; Job 21:12; 30:31)

ouch is a setting for a precious stone, not a cry of pain (Exodus 28:11, 13, 25)

paps *breasts* (Ezekiel 23:21; Luke 11:27; 23:29; Revelation 1:13)

passenger *traveler, passerby* (Proverbs 9:15; Ezekiel 39:11, 14–15)

peculiar denotes something of value (e.g., *special, personal possession*), not something odd or strange (Exodus 19:5; Deuteronomy 14:2; 26:18; Psalm 135:4; Ecclesiastes 2:8; Titus 2:14; 1 Peter 2:9)

peradventure *perhaps, maybe* (Genesis 18:24, 28–32; 24:5, 39; Exodus 32:30)

poll *cut, trim* hair (2 Samuel 14:26; Ezekiel 44:20; Micah 1:16)

port *gate, door* (2 Samuel 18:26; Mark 13:34), and **porter** *gatekeeper, doorkeeper* (Nehemiah 2:13; John 10:3); from French *porte*, "door, gate"

pottage *soup, stew* (Genesis 25:29–30, 34; 2 Kings 4:38–40; Haggai 2:12)

prevent *precede, anticipate* (Psalm 119:147; Matthew 17:25; Job 3:12; 41:11; Psalms 59:10; 88:13; 1 Thessalonians 4:15)

protest *affirm* (Genesis 43:3; 1 Corinthians 15:31). The term *Protestant* originally referred to those who affirmed a different belief than the Roman Catholic Church, but because they broke off from Catholicism, the term subsequently took on a connotation of rebellion.

prove *test* (Exodus 16:4; John 6:6)

publish *make known* (Deuteronomy 32:3; 1 Samuel 31:9; 2 Samuel 1:20; Nehemiah 8:15; Esther 1:20, 22; Isaiah 52:7; Jeremiah 4:5; 5:20; Mark 1:45; 5:20)

pulse *vegetables*. The term really denotes leguminous vegetables or their seeds. In Daniel 1:12, 16, it translates the Hebrew word meaning "seed." In 2 Samuel 17:28, it does not represent an underlying Hebrew term.

purpose is used verbally in KJV in the sense of to *plan* (1 Kings 5:5; 2 Chronicles 32:2; Ezra 4:5; Psalm 140:4; Acts 19:21; 20:3;

Romans 1:13). The idiom "on purpose" ("of purpose" in Ruth 2:16) therefore means "according to plan," or "as planned."

quick *alive* (Psalm 124:3; 2 Timothy 4:1); cf. **quicken,** *revive* (Psalms 71:20; 119:25, 37, 40; Romans 4:17; 8:11)

quit oneself *perform one's duties* (1 Samuel 4:9; 1 Corinthians 16:13)

ravin as noun, *prey* (Nahum 2:12); as a verb, *plunder, take prey* (Genesis 49:27); **ravening** *eager for prey* (Psalm 22:13; Ezekiel 22:25, 27; Matthew 7:15; Luke 11:39)

reins *kidneys,* often used figuratively to denote emotions or thoughts (Job 16:13; 19:27; Psalms 7:9; 16:7; 26:2; 73:21; 139:13; Jeremiah 11:20; Revelation 2:23)

rend (past tense **rent**) *tear, rip* (Genesis 37:29, 33–34; Exodus 39:23; Leviticus 10:6; 2 Samuel 3:31; John 19:24)

repent originally meant *to change one's mind, to rethink* (from French *penser,* "to think"), as in Hebrews 12:17. When KJV says that God "repented" (e.g., Genesis 6:6; 1 Chronicles 21:15), it means He changed His mind. When Moses called upon God to "repent," he was merely asking Him to change His mind, which God did (Exodus 32:12–14).

resort *come* (2 Chronicles 11:13; Nehemiah 4:20; Psalm 71:3; Mark 2:13; 10:1; John 10:41; 18:2, 20; Acts 16:13)

rest sometimes means *remain* (Joshua 3:13; Ecclesiastes 7:9; Romans 2:17)

rude means *unlearned, untaught,* not *discourteous* or *impolite* (2 Corinthians 11:6). In Joseph Smith's time, **rudeness** meant *harshness, savagery* (1 Nephi 18:9; 2 Nephi 2:1).

scholar *pupil, student.* The original meaning was *one who attends a school,* not *an expert* (1 Chronicles 25:8; Malachi 2:12).

scrip *moneybag, purse* (1 Samuel 17:40; Matthew 10:10)

season *a while, for a time,* can denote any period of time (Genesis 40:4; Joshua 24:7; 1 Chronicles 21:29; 2 Chronicles 15:3; Job 30:17; Proverbs 15:23; Ecclesiastes 3:1; Matthew 24:45)

secret sometimes refers to having someone's confidence (cf. "confidential" and "confide"). Thus, "the **secret** of the Lord" in Psalm 25:14 means having the Lord's confidence (cf. Amos 3:7).

seethe *boil* (Exodus 16:23; 23:19; 2 Kings 4:38; 1 Samuel 2:13; Ezekiel 24:5)

servant one of the most common terms in the KJV and denotes a *slave.* The word *slave* used in Jeremiah 2:14 does not reflect an underlying Hebrew word and was added by the KJV translators.

shambles *food market* (1 Corinthians 10:25)

sith *since* (Ezekiel 35:6)

sleight *trickery* (Ephesians 4:14)

slime *bitumen, tar* (Genesis 11:3; 14:10; Exodus 2:3)

sod *boil* (Genesis 25:29; 2 Chronicles 35:13); **sodden** means *boiled* (Exodus 12:9; Leviticus 6:28; Numbers 6:19; 1 Samuel 2:15; Lamentations 4:10)

sore often means *much, very* (Genesis 20:8; 31:30; 50:10; Exodus 14:10; Joshua 9:24)

supple *soften* (Ezekiel 16:4)

surfeiting *self-indulgence, selfishness* (Luke 21:34)

tabering *beating, drumming* (Nahum 2:7), from French *tambour,* "drum"

tale *number, count* (Exodus 5:8, 18; 1 Samuel 18:27), related to *toll, tell,* and *total.*[9] Cf. Genesis 15:5, where God says to Abraham, "Look now toward heaven, and tell the stars, if thou be able to number them."

target *shield* (1 Samuel 17:6; 1 Kings 10:16)

tarry *remain, stay* (Genesis 19:2; John 3:22; 21:22), sometimes means *delay* (Genesis 45:9)

temper *moisten* (Exodus 29:2; Ezekiel 46:14), as in "tempered steel," which is strengthened by being thrust into water after being hammered out

timbrel *tambourine* (Exodus 15:20; Judges 11:34; 2 Samuel 6:5; 1 Chronicles 13:8; Job 21:12; Psalm 68:25; 81:2; 149:3; 150:4); both words derive from French *tambour,* "drum"

travail *work, labor,* a French borrowing sometimes used in the sense of labor in childbirth (Genesis 38:27; Exodus 18:8; Numbers 20:14; Psalm 48:6; Ecclesiastes 2:23; Isaiah 23:4; 53:11; 54:1; John 16:21)

trow *suppose, think* (Luke 17:9)

try *test,* not *attempt* (Judges 7:4; Job 23:10; 2 Chronicles 32:31; Psalms 17:3; 26:2; 66:10; 139:23; Zechariah 13:9; 1 Corinthians 3:13), related to **trial,** as in 1 Peter 4:12

vintage *grape harvest* (Leviticus 26:5; Judges 8:2; Job 24:6; Isaiah 16:10; 24:13; 32:10; Jeremiah 48:32; Micah 7:1; Zechariah 11:2)

want usually means *lack* or *need* rather than *desire* (Deuteronomy 15:8; 28:48; Judges 18:10; 19:19–20; Job 31:19; Psalm 23:1; Proverbs 6:11; Luke 15:14)

well favoured *beautiful* (Genesis 29:17; 39:6; 41:2, 4, 18; Daniel 1:4; Nahum 3:4)

whence *from where* (Genesis 3:23; Genesis 16:8)[10]

wherefore is one of the most common words in KJV, usually denoting *why?* (i.e., "for what?")[11]

whither *to where* (Genesis 16:8; Ruth 1:16)

whole generally means *all, complete,* but in some cases means *healthy, healed* (Joshua 5:8; Job 5:18; Matthew 9:12, 21–22; John 5:4, 6, 9, 11, 14–15)

will as a stand-alone verb means *want, desire* (Matthew 8:2; 15:28; 19:21; 26:17; 26:39; John 21:22)

without often means *outside* or *outdoors* (Genesis 6:14; 9:22; 19:16; Exodus 26:35; 33:7; Leviticus 14:41; 1 Kings 6:29–30; Matthew 12:46–47; John 18:16)

wont *accustomed, habituated* (Exodus 21:29; Numbers 22:30; 1 Samuel 30:31; 2 Samuel 20:18; Daniel 3:19; Matthew 27:15; Mark 10:1; Luke 22:39; Acts 16:13)

wot (Genesis 21:26; Acts 3:17), **wotteth** (Genesis 39:8; Exodus 32:1, 23; Acts 7:40; Romans 11:2), **wit** (Exodus 2:4; Genesis

24:21; 2 Corinthians 8:1), and **wist** (Joshua 8:14; John 5:13; Luke 2:49) are all forms of a verb meaning *to know* (cf. wit, wise, wisdom). In Psalm 107:27, **wit** means *wisdom, knowledge*. Also deriving from the same verb are words like **witness** (one who knows) and **witless** (one who does not know).

would followed by a verb means *want to* (John 12:21)

wroth *angry* (Genesis 4:5–6; 31:36), related to **wrath,** *anger*

wrought *made, did* (Genesis 34:7; Exodus 10:2; 26:36; 27:16), related to **wright,** "maker," as in *wheelwright* (wheel maker), *cartwright* (cart maker), *wainwright* (wagon maker)

NOTES

1 A French borrowing used in the Book of Mormon but not the Bible is *adieu* (Jacob 7:27), "farewell," which is listed as an English word in Webster's 1828 dictionary. Another is *enfin*, "finally, in conclusion" (literally "in the end"), written "in fine" in English (1 Nephi 10:14; 22:23; 2 Nephi 2:15; 9:38; 28:28; Jarom 1:8; Omni 1:3; Alma 13:5; 24:1; 31:11; 36:14; 46:17; 48:22; 62:2; Helaman 12:2; 3 Nephi 1:17; 4 Nephi 1:14; Ether 13:17, 26).

2 When the Normans conquered Britain and became the upper class, they were the only ones who could afford to eat meat, so the French names of some animals (such as *boeuf*) came to be used in English to denote the meat deriving from those creatures. Thus, the French word *mouton*, meaning "sheep," became the English word *mutton*, while *poulet*, "chicken," came to be used in English (*pullet*) for a hen intended for cooking rather than laying eggs.

3 In the Job passage, it is paralleled by *den*.

4 The suffix *-el* denotes "small."

5 A cotton gin traps the seeds, separating them from the cotton.

6 In the book of Revelation, the term *glass* is used as in modern English (Revelation 4:6; 15:2; 21:18, 21).

7 When ghosts were said to "haunt" a place, it meant that they frequented it.

8 The Hebrew word rendered "hold" in most of these passages also underlies the site named Massada, a large mountaintop fortification overlooking the Dead Sea from the west. In 1 Samuel 22:3–4, we read that David took his parents for safety to the land of Moab on the opposite shore of the Dead Sea.

9 English words denoting counting often are also used in reference to telling. For example, *recount*, "tell" (literally "count again") is related to *count* and *account*. This feature was

borrowed from French.

10 In John 6:5, the Greek can also mean "how?" or "with what?"

11 In Shakespeare's *Romeo and Juliet,* when Juliet says, "Romeo, Romeo, wherefore art thou?" she was not asking where he was, but why he was Romeo, a member of a rival family.

CHAPTER V

~

Spelling Variations

Standardized spelling of English words was slow in coming. American English was standardized in the nineteenth century, mostly by Noah Webster and his successors, but British English often went a different direction—sometimes opting for the French spelling of borrowed words (e.g., *centre* vs. *center, theatre* vs. *theater,* etc.). What follows is a list of KJV words whose spelling has changed in modern English or whose form has otherwise changed over the years.

agone *ago* (1 Samuel 30:13)

bewray *betray* (Proverbs 27:16; 29:24; Isaiah 16:3; Matthew 26:72)

broid *braid, plait* (1 Timothy 2:9)

broider *embroider, to ornament* (Exodus 28:4; Ezekiel 16:10)

cloke *cloak* (Isaiah 59:17; Matthew 5:40; Luke 6:29; 2 Timothy 4:13)

clothes *cloths* (Luke 2:7, 12; 24:12), "cloth" being the origin of the term "clothe." Some KJV passages use "cloth" or "cloths."

cuckow *cuckoo* (Leviticus 11:16; Deuteronomy 14:15)

divers *diverse* (Matthew 24:7; Hebrew 1:1)

dure *endure, last* (Matthew 13:21), a borrowing from French *durer*, whence also English *during*

endue (Genesis 30:20) is the same as **endow** (Exodus 22:16) and usually denotes the brideprice paid to a man's intended father-in-law, though it can also denote any gift, especially from God (2 Chronicles 2:12–13; James 3:13). Compare Luke 24:49 with D&C 38:32, 38; 43:16; 95:8; 105:11–12, 18, 33; 110:9.[1]

ensample *example,* which is also used in KJV (John 13:15; Philippians 3:17; 2 Thessalonians 3:9)

felloe *felly* (the outside rim of a wheel; 1 Kings 7:33)

graff *graft* (Romans 11:17, 19, 23–24)

grave *engrave* (Exodus 28:9, 36; 1 Kings 7:36; 2 Chronicles 2:7, 14; 3:7). *Engrave* is also used in some KJV passages (Exodus 28:11; Zechariah 3:9; 2 Corinthians 3:7).

heretick *heretic, apostate* (Titus 3:10)

hoise *hoist* (Acts 27:40)

holpen *helped* (Psalms 83:8; 86:17; Isaiah 31:3; Daniel 11:34; Luke 1:54)

lade (and **laden**) *load* (Genesis 44:13; 45:17, 23; 1 Kings 12:11; Matthew 11:28; Luke 11:46); cf. **loaden** in Isaiah 46:1

milch milk (Genesis 32:15; 1 Samuel 6:7, 10)

minish *diminish* (Exodus 5:19; Psalm 107:39)

pill *peel* (Genesis 30:37–38)

plaister *plaster* (Leviticus 14:42–43, 48; Deuteronomy 27:2, 4; Daniel 5:5)

plat is used only once in reference to a piece of ground (2 Kings 9:26) and more often means *plait* (Matthew 27:29; Mark 15:17; John 19:2)

quit *acquit, absolve, free* (Exodus 21:19, 28; Joshua 2:20)

rereward *rearward* or *rearguard* (Numbers 10:25; Joshua 6:9, 13; 1 Samuel 29:2). Note that *ward* and *guard* are variants of the same word, with the same interchange found in English William, which derives from French Guillaume. Thus, to keep someone "in ward" (Genesis 40:3–4) is to keep him "under guard." To Isaiah, the Lord declared that he would go both before and behind (*rereward*) Israel (Isaiah 52:12; 58:8). The opposite of *rearward/rearguard* in English is *vanguard,* deriving from French *avant garde,* where *avant* means "before," hence the "front guard" or "forward."

resemble *compare* (Luke 13:18)

road *raid* (1 Samuel 27:10). The English words *ride, road,* and *raid* have a common origin.

shew *show.* Both words are pronounced alike, just as *sew* (clothing) and *sow* (seeds) are pronounced alike.

sope *soap* (Jeremiah 2:22; Malachi 3:2)

spue *spew, spit* (Leviticus 18:28; 20:22; Jeremiah 25:27; Revelation 3:16)

spunge *sponge* (Matthew 27:48; Mark 15:36; John 19:29)

stablish *establish* (2 Samuel 7:13; 1 Chronicles 17:12; 18:3; 2 Chronicles 7:18; Esther 9:21; Psalm 119:38; Romans 16:25; 1 Thessalonians 3:13; 2 Thessalonians 2:17; 3:3; James 5:8; 1 Peter 5:10), a French loan-word

taches *attachments* (Exodus 26:6, 11, 33; 35:11; 36:13, 18; 39:33), a borrowing from French

trode *trod*, past tense of *tread* (Judges 9:27; 20:43; 2 Kings 7:17, 20; 9:33; 14:9; 2 Chronicles 25:18; Luke 12:1)

twain *two* (1 Samuel 18:21; 2 Kings 4:33; Isaiah 6:2; Jeremiah 34:18; Ezekiel 21:19; Matthew 5:41; 19:5–6; 21:13; 27:51); cf. *twin*

whether is sometimes used in KJV in the sense of *which* (Judges 9:2; Ecclesiastes 11:6; Matthew 9:5; 21:31; 23:17, 19; 27:21; Mark 2:9; Luke 5:23; 22:27; Acts 1:24)

wine fat *wine vat* (Isaiah 63:2). A **fat** is a large vessel or tub (e.g., Joel 2:24; 3:13), and its modern equivalent is *vat*; cf. **pressfat** in Haggai 2:16.

NOTES

1 Christ told his apostles to remain in Jerusalem until they would be "endowed with power from on high," after which they could go to all nations to preach. This endowment came when the Holy Ghost fell on them, manifested by a strong wind and tongues of fire, on the day of Pentecost (Acts 2:1–4). The same manifestations occurred during the dedication of the Kirtland Temple in March 1836 (D&C 109:35–41; *History of the Church* 2:376, 428), and only after this time were the Twelve sent overseas to preach.

CHAPTER VI

Different Renderings of Hebrew and Greek Words

Because the translation of the KJV involved several committees and some 47 translators, the final product renders Hebrew words in a variety of ways, depending on the translator's personal preference. Here are some examples.

The Hebrew word *nepesh* is variously translated *soul* or *creature*. Indeed, the same Hebrew words underlie the description of Adam as a "living soul" (Genesis 2:7) and "living creature" denoting animals (Genesis 1:21, 24).

KJV uses the term *cormorant* to render two different Hebrew words, one of which (Isaiah 34:11; Zephaniah 2:14) is probably a pelican, while the other (Leviticus 11:17; Deuteronomy 14:17) is probably a true cormorant.

In the Old Testament, the English idiom *god forbid* underlies a Hebrew term meaning "it is profanation" (Genesis 44:2, 17), while in the New Testament it translates the Greek idiom meaning "let it not be" (Romans 3:4, 6, 31).

In England it was common to proclaim a new king by the expression "God save the king." The KJV translators used this in place of the Old Testament Hebrew idiom meaning "may the king live" (e.g., 1 Kings 1:25, 34, 39; 2 Kings 11:12).

The Hebrew words *elah* and *elon* are variously rendered "oak, terebinth, ash, teil, etc.," in the KJV.

Ambiguity in the English Text

Sometimes, words used by the KJV translators obscure the intent of the original text. This can be either because the English word has a different range of meaning than its Hebrew or Greek original or because the KJV word order is different from what one would expect in modern English.

For example, in Matthew 17:1, we read that "Jesus taketh Peter, James, and John his brother, and bringeth them up into an high mountain apart." Some readers have taken this as evidence that the Mount of Transfiguration must be "a mountain apart," or unconnected to nearby mountains, as is Mount Tabor, which stands alone as a large dome-shaped hill in the Jezreel Valley near Nazareth. However, the Greek text uses *kat'idian,* "by oneself," which is best rendered "privately," and refers to the fact that Jesus took the three apostles aside ("apart") to be alone with them. We can compare the wording of Matthew 14:23, where Jesus "went up into a mountain apart to pray" (i.e., to be alone), where the same Greek words are used.

Paul wrote that the resurrected Jesus "was seen of Cephas, then of the twelve" (1 Corinthians 15:5), leaving some Latter-day Saints to wonder if this means that Cephas (Peter) was "then (i.e., "at that time") of the twelve," prior to the organization of a First Presidency, or whether Christ was first seen by Peter, "then *(afterward)*" by the twelve. A quick check with the Greek shows that the original text uses the word *eita,* which is the subsequent "then," not the circumstantial "then." Hence, we should read "afterward."

The range of English words—especially particles—is not always paralleled in other languages. Therefore, one cannot arbitrarily assign any and all possible meanings of the English to a given Bible word. Rather, we must determine which Hebrew, Aramaic, or Greek word underlies it, and we must sometimes look at the syntax of the sentence in the original.

Borrowed Hebrew Idioms

Some Hebrew idioms have made their way into English. For example, in Numbers 22:4, the Hebrew word meaning "to lick" (with the tongue) refers to the defeat of an enemy. Because of this use, the English term *lick* came to have the same meaning as the Hebrew. ("My dad can lick your dad.") Another example comes from Job 19:20, which reads "I am escaped with the **skin of my teeth,**" which is a literal translation from the Hebrew. In modern English it would read "I have escaped by the skin of my teeth."

CHAPTER VII

～◠⌒～

Later Misunderstandings of Original Intent

On occasion the KJV translation is misunderstood by modern readers because of its antiquated language and because of literary devices that make better sense in Hebrew and Greek. For example, when Jesus told His disciples to pluck out one's eye and cut off one's hand (Matthew 5:29–30), this was only figurative. Or consider the fact that many English readers of the Bible think that Eve was intended to be a "help mate" for Adam, though the KJV actually calls her a "help meet" (i.e., suitable) for the man. The Hebrew word behind the KJV "meet" means "opposite, complementary, equal to."

Hyperbole

Hyperbole or exaggeration is frequent in the KJV Bible and is still used in English (for example, "I've told you a thousand times. . . ."). Thus, "the fish that got away" is always larger than the one brought home.

An example of hyperbole in the Old Testament is found in 1 Kings 12:10–11 (also 2 Chronicles 10:10–11), where Solomon's son Rehoboam tells the people, "My little *finger* shall be thicker than my father's loins. . . . My father hath chastised you with whips, but I will chastise you with scorpions." Here are some other examples of hyperbole in the Old Testament:

And there went forth a wind from the LORD, and
brought quails from the sea, and let them fall by the
camp, as it were a day's journey on this side, and as it
were a day's journey on the other side, round about the
camp, and as it were two cubits high upon the face of the
earth. (Numbers 11:31)

HEAR O Israel: Thou art to pass over Jordan this day, to
go in to possess nations greater and mightier than thyself,
cities great and fenced [walled] up to heaven.
(Deuteronomy 9:1)

Jesus also used hyperbole. For example, speaking of the
Jerusalem temple, he said, "There shall not be left here one
stone upon another, that shall not be thrown down" (Matthew
24:2). Bible readers visiting Jerusalem are surprised to find that
some three-quarters of the foundation of the wall that
surrounded Herod's temple remains in place (including three of
its four corners), and that some portions of the wall retain as
much as three-fourths of their original height. Knowing this
fact, if one thinks only in terms of modern literal English, one
would conclude that this part was mistranslated, but if one
considers hyperbole as a normal part of speech in Christ's day, it
becomes clear that he was merely saying that the temple would
be destroyed.

On another occasion Jesus declared, "It is easier for a camel to
go through the eye of a needle, than for a rich man to enter into
the kingdom of God" (Matthew 19:24). Many centuries later,
Christians reinterpreted the "eye of a needle" as referring to a
smaller door in the large city gates through which a camel could
enter, but only if its burden of wares was removed. But such gates
did not exist in Christ's time and only came into use with the
Crusades of the Middle Ages. Christ was merely speaking hyper-
bolically. Indeed, we have a parallel to his statement in the

Talmud (*Baba Metzia* 38b), where the rabbis spoke of an elephant going through the eye of a needle, which is considerably more hyperbolic than Jesus' statement about the camel. But we have further evidence of the hyperbolic nature of Christ's statement in the fact that he also said, "Ye blind guides, which strain at a gnat, and swallow a camel" (Matthew 23:24).

Hebrew and Greek Words Transliterated in KJV

Sometimes, the KJV translators were unaware of the meaning of a word in the original Hebrew and Greek text, so they merely transliterated the foreign word rather than translating it into English. A good example is the word *baptize*, from the Greek word meaning "dip" or "immerse." Because immersion had been discontinued for centuries in western Christianity, the translators avoided using the real meaning of the word and used instead the Greek term, thus obscuring its meaning. (This is a feature of other Bible translations as well, including those made into other European languages.)

In some New Testament passages, where the Greek text employs words that are Aramaic, the KJV translators retained the transliterated words. In some of these cases, the text says that the words are Hebrew, which is what Aramaic was called in Christ's day.[1] For example, in Matthew 27:46, the dying Christ cried out, *"Eli, Eli, lama sabachthani?"* that is to say, "My God, my God, why hast thou forsaken me?" These are the opening words of the Aramaic version of Psalm 22:1.[2] When raising a girl from the dead, Jesus said, *Talitha cumi,* Aramaic for "young woman [*damsel* in KJV], arise" (Mark 5:41).

Jesus gave the Aramaic name *Kepha,* meaning "stone," to his chief apostle, Simon. While most of the New Testament calls him Peter, from the Greek word for "stone" (petra), some passages call him Cephas, the Greek transliteration of the Aramaic word (John 1:42; 1 Corinthians 1:12; 3:22; 9:5; 15:5; Galatians 2:9).

Here is a list of some of the Aramaic, Hebrew, and Greek words that the KJV translators retained in transliterated form:

abaddon loss, perdition. Though used in a New Testament Greek text, it is Hebrew in origin. The Greek term, used in the same verse, is *apollyon*. (Revelation 9:11)

algum or **almug** a type of tree (2 Chronicles 2:8, etc.; 1 Kings 10:11)

Alpha and Omega a title of Christ, using the first and last letters of the Greek alphabet (Revelation 1:8, 11; 21:6; 22:13)

Anathema Maranatha the first term is Greek for *cursed*; the second, *maran atha,* "Lord come," is Aramaic (1 Corinthians 16:22)

bath a liquid measure (Isaiah 5:10; Ezekiel 45:10–11, 14)

bdellium (from Hebrew *bedolach*) thought variously to be a gum/resin, a gemstone, or a pearl (Genesis 2:12; Numbers 11:7)

behemoth generally considered to be a mythological animal (Job 40:15)

beryl probably aquamarine. The Greek word was borrowed by English and is also used in the KJV Old Testament (Revelation 21:20).

cab a dry measure (2 Kings 6:25)

camphire henna or an aromatic shrub (Song of Solomon 1:14; 4:13)

cherub (plural **cherubim**)[3] an Akkadian word borrowed by Hebrew and denoting winged creatures such as those seen in the heavenly visions of Ezekiel. See **seraph** below.

chrysolite a precious stone (Revelation 21:20)

chrysoprasus probably a variety of agate (Revelation 21:20)

cor a dry measure (Ezekiel 45:14)

ephah a dry measure (Exodus 16:36; Isaiah 5:10; Ezekiel 45:10–11, 13; etc.)

ephod a priestly garment, borrowed from Egyptian (Exodus 25:7; 1 Samuel 22:18; etc.)

Gabbatha the Aramaic term denoting a raised pavement of stones (John 19:13)

galbanum a spice (Exodus 30:34)

Golgotha the "place of a skull," where Christ was crucified, is the Aramaic word for "skull" (Matthew 27:33; Mark 15:22; John 19:17), cognate to the Hebrew *gulgolet* (Judges 9:53).[4] Luke 23:33 has the Greek *kranion,* "skull, cranium," which KJV renders *Calvary,* a term borrowed from Latin.

gopher wood, perhaps cypress, fir, or cedar (Genesis 6:14)

heresy false teaching, apostasy. The Greek word *hairesis* was in use from the time of the apostles and was adopted into many of the languages spoken by Christians (Acts 24:14; 1 Corinthians 11:19; Galatians 5:20; 2 Peter 2:1)

hin a liquid measure (Exodus 29:40)

homer a dry measure (Leviticus 27:16; Isaiah 5:10; Ezekiel 45:11, 13–14)

jacinth perhaps sapphire or ligure (Revelation 9:17; 21:20)

jasper a stone whose name was borrowed from Hebrew (Exodus 28:20; 39:13)

leviathan is sometimes not transliterated and is wrongly rendered "mourning" in Job 3:8. In Job 41:1–34, it is perhaps a crocodile, while in Psalm 104:26 it may refer to a whale. See Isaiah 27:1. Its occurrence in Psalm 74:14 (borrowed from an old Canaanite poem) is probably figurative.

log a liquid capacity measure, borrowed from Egyptian (Leviticus 14:10, 12, 15, 21, 24)

maneh a weight (Ezekiel 45:12); in the Aramaic of Daniel 5:25–26, it is *mene*

manna from Hebrew *man hu'*, "What is it?" (Exodus 16:15, 31, 35; John 6:31, 49, 58; etc.)

omer a dry measure (Exodus 16:16, 18, 32–33, 36)

Passover is partially based on the Hebrew term *Pesach,* though both *pass* and *over* are English terms (Exodus 12:11–12, 21, 27, 43, 48). The Hebrew term is rendered *Pascha* in the Greek New Testament, where KJV usually translates it as *Passover* (Matthew 26:2, 17–19), though in Acts 12:4 it is rendered *Easter.*

sapphire actually a Hebrew word borrowed into English, though it may actually denote another precious stone such as the related emerald or lapis lazuli (Exodus 28:18; Ezekiel 28:13; Revelation 21:19)

sackcloth from Hebrew *saq,* denoting a rough cloth worn while mourning (frequent in Old Testament)

sardine an orange-red chalcedony (Revelation 4:3)

sardius a precious stone (Revelation 21:20)

shekel a weight (Genesis 23:15); in the Aramaic of Daniel 5:25–27, it is *tekel*

sheraphim denoting winged creatures seen in Isaiah's heavenly vision (Isaiah 6:2, 6)[5]

shittah probably the acacia tree (Isaiah 41:19). Note the plural form *shittim* wood (Exodus 25:5, 10, 13; Numbers 25:1).

sycamine a type of mulberry tree (Luke 17:6)

teraphim thought to be small idols (Judges 17:5; 18:14, 17f, 28; Hosea 3:4)

topaz which English has borrowed from the Greek text (Revelation 21:20)

urim and **thummim** oracles, whose meaning has been much disputed[6] (Exodus 28:30; Ezra 2:63; etc.)

Mythological and Unknown Creatures in KJV

Unaware of the meaning of some Hebrew words denoting animals known in the Near East, the KJV translators rendered them as the names of mythological animals.

cockatrice renders a Hebrew word denoting a species of serpent. The English term refers to a serpent said to have hatched from a cock's egg (Isaiah 11:8; 14:29; 59:5).

dragon is Hebrew *tannin,* variously thought to denote a poisonous serpent, a crocodile, or a jackal (Psalm 91:13; Isaiah 27:1; etc.)

satyr is probably a hairy animal, the word being related to the Hebrew word for "hair" (Isaiah 13:21; 34:14)

unicorn meaning "one horn," is a translation of Hebrew *re'em,* perhaps a wild ox. In Isaiah 34:7, where KJV has *unicorn,* the Joseph Smith translation has *reem* (Numbers 23:22; Psalm 22:21; etc.).

Weights, Measures, and Coinage

Often, the KJV translators decided to render Greek words for weight, measures, and coins as English terms known to their orders. Unfortunately, some of these words are no longer used in English, confusing matters even more. Here are some examples.

farthing In Matthew 10:29 and Luke 12:6, this word is used in place of Greek *assarion,* a coin that is a hundredth of a *denarius.* In Matthew 5:26 and Mark 12:42, it replaces Greek *kodrantes,* from Latin *quadrans,* which is half an *assarion.*

firkin Greek *metretes,* probably same as Hebrew *bath,* a liquid measure

furlong is a Greek *stadion* (Luke 24:13). Both are an eighth of a mile, so the KJV translators made a good choice.

mite referring to something small (as the insect of the same name), replaces Greek *lepton,* a small copper coin (Mark 12:42; Luke 12:59; 21:2)

penny denotes Greek *denarion,* from Latin *denarius* (Matthew 20:2, 9f, 13; John 6:7; Revelation 6:6); plural *pence* (Matthew 18:28)

pound renders Greek *lira* (from Latin *libra*) in the New Testament (John 12:3; 19:39) and Hebrew *maneh,* a weight, in some Old Testament passages (1 Kings 10:17; Ezra 2:69; Nehemiah 7:71f); in others (Luke 19:13–25), it renders the Greek equivalent, *mina,* referring to money.

A notable exception is the use of *silverling* in Isaiah 7:23 to denote a small piece of silver (*kesef* in the Hebrew original).

Rendering of Other Misunderstood Words

The difficulty in rendering or representing terms peculiar to one culture into the language of another culture is evident in the fact that the KJV translators often used English terms to denote Hebrew or Greek terms whose meaning was unknown to their readers. For example, Isaiah 3:18–24 lists various items of clothing and jewelry worn anciently but whose meaning was lost over time. In this case, the KJV translators applied terms known for women's apparel in their day but many unknown in our modern society.

This procedure was particularly applied to military and leadership titles. Thus, we have the following:

serjeant as a rendering of the Greek translation of the Roman *lictor* (Acts 16:35, 38)

lieutenant a borrowed French word literally meaning "place (*lieu*) holding (*tenant*)," to denote a Persian provincial governor's title written in Hebrew letters (Ezra 8:36; Esther 3:12; 8:9; 9:3)

sheriff as a rendering of an Aramaic term for a magistrate (Daniel 3:2–3)

duke as the title of various Edomite rulers (Genesis 36:15–19, 21, 29–30, 40–43; 1 Chronicles 1:51–54)

prince is the word used by KJV to translate Hebrew *sar,* which denotes military or political leaders serving under a king. Some KJV passages render it *captain,* which is also the way the Hebrew *nagid* ("leader") is often translated.

In some cases, the titles were Akkadian (Babylonian) rather than Hebrew and their meanings unknown to the KJV translators (and perhaps the Bible writers themselves), who took them to be names rather than titles (see 2 Kings 18:17, 19, 26–28, 37; 19:4, 8; Isaiah 20:1; 36:2, 4, 11–13, 22; 37:4, 8; Jeremiah 39:3, 13). *Tirshatha,* the title of Nehemiah, appointed governor of the Persian province of Judea in the late sixth century B.C., was also left untranslated (Ezra 2:63; Nehemiah 7:65, 70; 8:9; 10:1).

Other Problems in Understanding the KJV

The way we read the KJV Bible is sometimes influenced by outside factors, such as motion pictures and watered-down children's books about Bible stories. Some misconceptions have been with us for a long time. A few examples will illustrate.

One common misconception is that Jesus taught a multitude of people when He delivered the Sermon on the Mount. But the Bible says that He went on the mount to get away from the multitude. "And there followed him great multitudes of people from Galilee, and from Decapolis, and from Jerusalem, and from Judæa, and from beyond Jordan. And seeing the multitude, he went up into a mountain: and when he was set, his disciples came unto him: And he opened his mouth, and taught them" (Matthew 4:25–5:2).

There are Old Testament passages that have God speaking in the plural, as if someone else were with Him: "Let *us* make man in *our* image" (italics added; Genesis 1:26). "The man is become as one of *us,* to know good and evil" (italics added; Genesis 3:22, confirming the truth Satan mingled with a lie in verse 5). Those who argue that this is a "plural of majesty" seem totally unaware of biblical usage, since this kind of plural, used in reference to European monarchs, is unknown in the Bible. Indeed, throughout the Old Testament, God, as well as the king, is addressed as "thou" (from the Hebrew second person masculine *singular* pronoun), and always speaks of himself as "I" rather than "we," while verbs and adjectives associated with God are in the *singular* rather than the plural form in the Hebrew original.

In KJV, the term *witch* or *sorceress,* its masculine equivalent *sorcerer,* and the abstract nouns *witchcraft* and *sorcery* are sometimes listed with other sins, suggesting that it denotes a fortune-teller or false prophet (Exodus 7:11; Deuteronomy 18:10–11; 2 Chronicles 33:6; Isaiah 47:9, 12; Jeremiah 27:9–10; Daniel 2:2; Micah 5:12; Acts 8:9–11; 13:6, 8; Revelation 18:23; 3 Nephi 21:16; Mormon 1:19; 2:10). But some passages list the *witch* with sexual sins, suggesting that it sometimes denoted people engaged in illicit sexual activities (Exodus 22:16–19; 2 Kings 9:22; Isaiah 57:3–4; Nahum 3:4; Malachi 3:5; Galatians 5:19–20; Revelation 9:21; 21:8; 22:15; D&C 63:17; 76:103).[7]

NOTES

1   Aramaic and Hebrew are sister languages employing the same alphabet in Christ's day. Jews exiled to Babylon adopted Aramaic in place of Hebrew as their own, though they retained some sacred texts (including the Bible) in Hebrew.

2   Mark 15:34 renders it *Eloi, Eloi, lama sabachthani.*

3   Though the *-im* suffix denotes masculine plural in Hebrew, the KJV translators also added the English plural suffix *-s,* giving us *cherubims.*

4   In linguistics, words are cognate if they are similar in pronunciation and meaning and derive from related languages (in this case, Hebrew and Aramaic).

5   As with *cherubim,* the KJV translators retained both the Hebrew and English plural suffixes. Scholars are divided on the meaning of the term. It may derive from the word *saraph,* which means "burning" and is also the name of a poisonous serpent. While the first (1830) edition of the Book of Mormon retained the KJV spelling, later editions omitted the English plural marker in the quotes from Isaiah 6 (2 Nephi 16:2, 6).

6   For a discussion, see John A. Tvedtnes, "Egyptian Etymologies for Biblical Religious Paraphernalia," in Sarah I. Groll (ed.), *Egyptological Studies (Scripta Hierosolymitana,* Vol. 28; Jerusalem: Magnes Press of the Hebrew University, 1982).

7   A different Hebrew word is rendered *witchcraft* in 1 Samuel 15:23, where it seems not to suggest either false prophecy or sexual sin.

Afterword

From the time of its first printing in 1611, the KJV has been the major Bible for speakers of English. Over the past two centuries, it has been the official English language Bible of The Church of Jesus Christ of Latter-day Saints.

Readers acquainted with the plays and sonnets of Shakespeare (who was nearly a contemporary of King James) are undoubtedly more comfortable with the language of the KJV than those who read only modern books.

Those who read the KJV Bible regularly can also become acquainted with its language. While this present book is designed to help people better understand the older English found in the KJV, its lessons will be most useful to those who turn to the Bible often. Because there are many "King Jamesisms" in the other standard works of the Church (often quoting KJV), it will be of assistance in reading and understanding them as well.

While other Bible versions may be easier to read than the King James Version, in doctrinal matters latter-day revelation supports the King James Version in preference to other English translations. All of the Presidents of the Church, beginning with the Prophet Joseph Smith, have supported the King James Version by encouraging its continued use in the Church. In light of all the above, it is the English language Bible used by The Church of Jesus Christ of Latter-day Saints.

We encourage all members to have their own copies of the complete standard works and to use them prayerfully in regular personal and family study, and in Church meetings and assignments.

—First Presidency policy statement, *Ensign,* August 1992

Appendix

The preface to the 1611 edition of the King James version of the Bible is enlightening, for it deals with translation issues that some modern Christians ignore, believing that God guided the entire process, thus leaving the KJV text inerrant. The preface also gives insights into the history behind the KJV and notes some doctrinal issues. It is regrettable that the preface is no longer published with the KJV itself, except for a large, expensive pulpit Bible that has been in print since 1821. It was included as an appendix in the 1935 edition, which marked the 400th anniversary of Coverdale's Bible. In the version that follows, the spelling of the original has been modernized (except for bracketed notes that were marginal notes in the 1611 edition), and footnotes have been added to explain some terms.

THE TRANSLATORS
TO THE READER
THE BEST THINGS HAVE BEEN CULMINATED[1]

ZEAL to promote the common good, whether it be by devising anything ourselves, or revising that which hath been laboured by others, deserveth certainly much respect and esteem, but yet findeth but cold entertainment in the world. It is welcomed with suspicion instead of love, and with emulation[2] instead of thanks: and if there be any hole left for cavil[3] to enter, (and cavil, if it do not find a hole, will make one) it is sure to be misconstrued, and in danger to be condemned. This will easily be granted by as many as know story,[4] or have any experience. For, was there ever anything projected, that savoured any way of newness or renewing, but the same endured many a storm of gainsaying, or opposition? A man would think that civility, wholesome laws, learning and eloquence, synods, and Church-maintenance, (that we speak of no more things of this kind) should be as safe as a sanctuary, and [exw beloiV] out of shot, as they say, that no man would lift up the heel, no, nor dog move his tongue against the motioners of them. For by the first, we are distinguished from brute-beasts led with sensuality: by the second, we are bridled and restrained from outrageous behaviour, and from doing of injuries, whether by fraud or by violence: by the third, we are enabled to inform and reform others, by the light and feeling that we have attained unto ourselves: briefly, by the fourth being brought together to a parle[5] face to face, we sooner compose our differences than by writings, which are endless: and lastly, that the Church be sufficiently provided for, is so agreeable to good reason and conscience, that those mothers are holden to be less cruel, that kill their children as soon as they are born, than those nursing fathers and mothers (wheresoever they be) that withdraw from them who hang upon their breasts (and upon whose breasts again themselves do hang to receive the spiritual and sincere milk of the word) livelihood and support fit for their estates. Thus it is apparent, that these things which we speak of are of most necessary use, and therefore that none, either without absurdity can speak against them, or without note of wickedness can spurn against them.

ANACHARSIS WITH OTHERS

Yet for all that, the learned know that certain worthy men have been brought to untimely death for none other fault, but for seeking to reduce their countrymen to good order and discipline: and that in some commonweals [Locri] it was made a capital crime, once to motion the making of a new law for the abrogating of an old, though the same were most pernicious: and that certain, [Cato the elder.] which would be counted pillars of the State, and patterns of virtue and prudence, could not be brought for a long time to give way to good letters and refined speech, but bare themselves as averse from them, as from rocks or boxes of poison: and fourthly, that he was no babe, but a great clerk, [Gregory the Divine.] that gave forth (and in writing to remain to posterity) in passion peradventure, but yet he gave forth, that he had not seen any profit to come by any synod or meeting of the clergy, but rather the contrary: and lastly, against Church maintenance and allowance, in such sort as the ambassadors and messengers of the great King of kings should be furnished, it is not unknown what a fiction or fable (so it is esteemed, and for no better by the reporter himself, [Nauclerus.] though superstitious) was devised: namely, that at such time as the professors and teachers of Christianity in the Church of Rome, then a true Church, were liberally endowed, a voice forsooth was heard from heaven, saying, Now is poison poured down into the Church, etc. Thus not only as oft as we speak, as one saith, but also as oft as we do anything of note or consequence, we subject ourselves to everyone's censure, and happy is he that is least tossed upon the tongues; for utterly to escape the snatch of them it is impossible. If any man conceit that this is the lot and portion of the meaner sort only, and that princes are privileged by their high estate, he is deceived. As *the sword devoureth as well one as the other*, as it is in *Samuel*; [2 Sam. 11:25] nay, as the great commander charged his soldiers in a certain battle to strike at no part of the enemy, but at the face; and as the King of *Syria* [1 Kings 22:31] commanded his chief captains *to fight neither with small nor great, save only against the King of Israel*: so it is too true, that envy striketh most spitefully at the fairest, and at the chiefest. *David* was a worthy prince, and no man to be compared to him for his first deeds, and yet for as worthy an act as ever he did (even for bringing back the ark of God in solemnity) he was scorned and scoffed at by his own wife. [2 Sam. 6:16] *Solomon* was greater than *David*, though not in virtue, yet in power: and by his power and wisdom he built a temple to the Lord, such a one as was the glory of the land of Israel, and the wonder of the whole world. But was that his magnificence liked of by all? We doubt of it. Otherwise, why do they lay it in his son's dish, and call unto him for [seisacqeian] easing of the burden? *Make*, say they, *the grievous servitude of thy father, and his sore yoke, lighter.* [1 Kings 12:4] Belike he had charged them with some levies, and troubled them with some carriages; hereupon they raise up a tragedy, and wish in their heart the temple had never been built. So hard a thing it is to please all, even when we please God best, and do seek to approve ourselves to everyone's conscience.

THE HIGHEST PERSONAGES HAVE BEEN CALUMNATED

If we will descend to later times, we shall find many the like examples of such kind, or rather unkind, acceptance. The first Roman emperor [C. Cæsar. Plutarch][6] did never do a more pleasing deed to the learned, nor more profitable to posterity, for conceiving the record of times in true supputation,[7] than when he corrected the Calendar, and ordered the year according to the course of the sun: and yet this was imputed to him for novelty, and arrogancy, and procured to him great obloquy.[8] So the first christened[9] emperor [Constantine.] (at the leastwise that openly professed the faith himself, and allowed others to do the like) for strengthening the empire at his great charges, and providing for the Church, as he did, got for his labour the name *pupillus,* [Aurel. Victor.] as who would say, a wasteful prince, that had need of a guardian, or overseer. So the best christened emperor, [Theodosius.] for the love that he bare unto peace, thereby to enrich both himself and his subjects, and because he did not seek war but find it, was judged [Zosimus.] to be no man at arms, (though indeed he excelled in feats of chivalry,[10] and shewed so much when he was provoked) and condemned for giving himself to his ease and to his pleasure. To be short, the most learned emperor of former times, [Justinian.] (at the least, the greatest politician) what thanks had he for cutting off the superfluities of the laws, and digesting them into some order and method? This, that he hath been blotted by some to be an epitomist,[11] that is, one that extinguished worthy whole volumes, to bring his abridgements into request. This is the measure that hath been rendered to excellent princes in former times, even, *cum benè facerent, malè audire,* for their good deeds to be evil spoken of. Neither is there any likelihood that envy and malignity[12] died and were buried with the ancient. No, no, the reproof of *Moses* taketh hold of most ages: *You are risen up in your father's stead, an increase of sinful men.* [Num. 32:14] *What is that that hath been done? that which shall be done: and there is no new thing under the sun,* [Eccl. 1:9] saith the wise man. And *S.*[13] *Stephen, As your fathers did, so do you.* [Acts 7:51]

HIS MAJESTY'S CONSTANCY, NOTWITHSTANDING CULMINATION, FOR THE SURVEY OF THE ENGLISH TRANSLATIONS

This, and more to this purpose, his Majesty that now reigneth, (and long and long may he reign, and his offspring for ever, *himself and children, and children's children always*) [Αυτου, και παιδε και παιδων παντοτε παιδε.] knew full well, according to the singular wisdom given unto him by God, and the rare learning and experience that he hath attained unto; namely, that whosoever attempteth anything for the public (specially if it pertain to religion, and to the opening and clearing of the word of God) the same setteth himself upon a stage to be glouted upon by every evil eye, yea, he casteth himself headlong upon pikes, to be gored by every sharp tongue. For he that meddleth with men's religion in any part meddleth with their custom, nay, with their freehold; and though they find no content in that which they have, yet they cannot abide to hear of altering. Notwithstanding his royal heart was not daunted or discouraged for this or that colour, but stood resolute, *as a statue immoveable, and an anvil not easy to be beaten into plates,* as one saith; [Suidas. ωσπερ τισ ανδριαυ απεριτρεπτο΄ και ακμων ανηλατο ΄.] he knew who had chosen him to be a soldier, or rather a captain, and being assured that the course which he intended made much for the glory of God, and the building up of his Church, he would not suffer it to be broken off for whatsoever speeches or practices. It doth certainly belong unto kings, yea, it doth specially belong unto them, to have care of religion, yea, to know it aright, yea, to profess it zealously, yea, to promote it to the uttermost of their power. This is their glory before all nations which mean well, and this will bring unto them a far most excellent weight of glory in the day of the Lord Jesus. For the Scripture saith not in vain, *Them that honour me, I will honour;* [1 Sam. 2:30] neither was it a vain word that *Eusebius* [qeosebeia, *Eusebius lib. 10 cap. 8.*] delivered long ago, that piety towards God was the weapon, and the only weapon, that both preserved *Constantine's* person and avenged him of his enemies.

THE PRAISE OF THE HOLY SCRIPTURES

But now what piety without truth? what truth (what saving truth) without the word of God? what word of God (whereof we may be sure) without the Scripture? The Scriptures we are commanded to search (John 5:39; Isa. 8:20). They are commended that searched and studied them (Acts 17:11 and 8:28, 29). They are reproved that were unskilful in them, or slow to believe them (Matt. 22:29; Luke 24:25). They can make us wise unto salvation (2 Tim. 3:15). If we be ignorant, they will instruct us; if out of the way, they will bring us home; if out of order, they will reform us; if in heaviness, comfort us; if dull, quicken us; if cold, inflame us. *Tolle, lege; tolle, lege:* [*S. August. confess. lib. 8. cap. 12.*] Take up and read, take up and read the Scriptures, (for unto them was the direction) it was said unto *S. Augustine* by a supernatural voice. [*S. August. de utilit. credendi, cap. 6.*] *Whatsoever is in the Scriptures, believe me,* saith the same *S. Augustine, is high and divine; there is verily truth, and a doctrine most fit for the refreshing and renewing of men's minds, and truly so tempered, that every one may draw from thence that which is sufficient for him, if he come to draw with a devout and pious mind, as true religion requireth.* Thus *S. Augustine.* And *S. Hierome*[14]: *Ama scripturas, et amabit te sapientia,* etc. [*S. Hieronym. ad Demetriad.*] Love the Scriptures, and wisdom will love thee. And *S. Cyril* against *Julian;* [*S. Cyril 7 contra Julianum.*] *Even boys that are bred up in the Scriptures, become most religious,* etc. But what mention we three or four uses of the Scripture, whereas whatsoever is to be believed or practised, or hoped for, is contained in them? or three or four sentences of the Fathers, since whosoever is worthy the name of a Father, from Christ's time downward, hath likewise written not only of the riches, but also of the perfection of the Scripture? [*Tertul. advers. Hermo.*] *I adore the fullness of the Scripture,* saith *Tertullian* against *Hermogenes.* And again, [*Tertul. de carne Christi.*] to *Apelles* an heretick of the like stamp, he saith: *I do not admit that which thou bringest in* (or concludest) *of thine own* (head or store, *de tuo*) without Scripture. So Saint *Justin Martyr* before him: [*Justin.* προτρεπτ. προ' ελλην. οιον τε.] *We must know by all means,* saith he, *that it is not lawful* (or possible) *to learn* (anything) *of God or of right piety, save only out of the*

Prophets, who teach us by divine inspiration. So Saint *Basil* after *Tertullian:* [*S. Basil.* περι πιζεω'. υπερηφανια' κατηγορια.] *It is a manifest falling away from the Faith, and a fault of presumption, either to reject any of those things that are written, or to bring in* (upon the head of them, epeisagein) *any of those things that are not written.* We omit to cite to the same effect *S. Cyril* B. of *Jerusalem,* in his 4 *Cataches.* Saint *Hierome* against *Helvidius,* Saint *Augustine* in his third book against the letters of *Petilian,* and in very many other places of his works. Also we forbear to descend to latter Fathers, because we will not weary the reader. The Scriptures then being acknowledged to be so full and so perfect, how can we excuse ourselves of negligence, if we do not study them? of curiosity, if we be not content with them? Men talk much of ειρεσιωνη, [Ειρεσιωνη συκα φερει, και πιονα' αρτου', και μελι εν κοτυλη, και ελαιον, etc. An olive bow wrapped about with wool, whereupon did hang figs, and bread, and honey in a pot, and oil.] how many sweet and goodly things it had hanging on it; of the Philosopher's stone, that it turneth copper into gold; of *Cornucopia,* that it had all things necessary for food in it; of *Panacca* the herb, that it was good for all diseases; of *Catholicon* the drug, that it is instead of all purges; of *Vulcan's* armour, that it was an armour of proof against all thrusts, and all blows, etc. Well, that which they falsely or vainly attributed to these things for bodily good, we may justly and with full measure ascribe unto the Scripture, for spiritual. It is not only an armour, but also a whole armoury of weapons, both offensive and defensive; whereby we may save ourselves and put the enemy to flight.[15] It is not an herb, but a tree, or rather a whole paradise of trees of life, which bring forth fruit every month, and the fruit thereof is for meat, and the leaves for medicine.[16] It is not a pot of *Manna,* or a cruse of oil, which were for memory only, or for a meal's meat or two, but as it were a shower of heavenly bread sufficient for a whole host, be it never so great; and as it were a whole cellar full of oil vessels;

whereby all our necessities may be provided for and our debts discharged. In a word, it is a panary[17] of wholesome food, against fenowed[18] traditions; a physician's shop [κοινον ιατρειον. *S. Basil. in Psal. primum.*] (Saint *Basil* calleth it) of preservatives against poisoned heresies; a pandect[19] of profitable laws against rebellious sprits; a treasury of most costly jewels against beggarly rudiments; finally, a fountain of most pure water springing up unto everlasting life. And what marvel? the original thereof being from heaven, not from earth; the author being God, not man; the inditer,[20] the Holy Spirit, not the wit of the Apostles or Prophets; the penmen, such as were sanctified from the womb, and endued[21] with a principal portion of God's Spirit; the matter, verity, piety, purity, uprightness; the form, God's word, God's testimony, God's oracles, the word of truth, the word of salvation, etc.; the effects, light of understanding, stableness of persuasion, repentance from dead works, newness of life, holiness, peace, joy in the Holy Ghost; lastly, the end and reward of the study thereof, fellowship with the Saints, participation of the heavenly nature,[22] fruition of an inheritance immortal, undefiled, and that never shall fade away. Happy is the man that delighteth in the Scripture, and thrice happy that meditateth in it day and night.

TRANSLATION NECESSARY

But how shall men meditate in that, which they cannot understand? How shall they understand that which is kept close in an unknown tongue? as it is written, *Except I know the power of the voice, I shall be to him that speaketh, a Barbarian, and he that speaketh, shall be a Barbarian to me.* [1 Cor. 14][23] The Apostle excepteth no tongue; not Hebrew the ancientest, not Greek the most copious, not Latin the finest. Nature taught a natural man to confess, that all of us in those tongues which we do not understand, are plainly deaf; we may turn the deaf ear unto them. The *Scythian* counted the *Athenian*, whom he did not understand, barbarous; [*Clem. Alex. 1 Strom.*] so the *Roman* did the *Syrian,* and the *Jew* (even *S. Hierome* himself called the Hebrew tongue barbarous, belike because it was strange to so many:) [S. Hieronym. Damaso.] so the Emperor of *Constantinople* [*Michael. Theophili fil.*] calleth the *Latin* tongue, barbarous, though Pope *Nicolas* do storm at it: [2. Tom. Concil. ex edit. Petri Crab.] so the *Jews* long before *Christ* called all other nations, *Lognazim,* which is little better than barbarous. Therefore as one complaineth, that always in the Senate of Rome, [Cicero 5 de finibus.] there was one or other that called for an interpreter: so lest the Church be driven to the like exigent, it is necessary to have translations in a readiness. Translation it is that openeth the window, to let in the light; that breaketh the shell, that we may eat the kernel; that putteth aside the curtain, that we may look into the most holy place;[24] that removeth the cover of the well, that we may come by the water, even as *Jacob* rolled away the stone from the mouth of the well, by which means the flocks of *Laban* were watered [Gen. 29:10]. Indeed, without translation into the vulgar tongue, the unlearned are but like children at *Jacob's* well (which was deep) [John 4:11] without a bucket or something to draw with: or as that person mentioned by *Isaiah*, to whom when a sealed book was delivered, with this motion, *Read this, I pray thee*, he was fain to make this answer, *I cannot, for it is sealed.* [Isa. 29:11]

THE TRANSLATION OF THE OLD TESTAMENT
OUT OF THE HEBREW INTO GREEK

While God would be known only in *Jacob,* and have his Name great in *Israel,* and in none other place, while the dew lay on *Gideon's* fleece only, and all the earth besides was dry; [*See S. August. lib. 12. contra Faust. c. 32.*] then for one and the same people, which spake all of them the language of *Canaan,* that is,

Hebrew, one and the same original in *Hebrew* was sufficient. But when the fullness of time drew near, that the Sun of righteousness, the Son of God, should come into the world, whom God ordained to be a reconciliation through faith in his blood, not of the *Jew* only, but also of the *Greek,* yea, of all them that were scattered abroad; then, lo, it pleased the Lord to stir up the spirit of a *Greek* prince (*Greek* for descent and language), even of *Ptolomy Philadelph,* King of *Egypt,* to procure the translating of the Book of God out of *Hebrew* into *Greek.* This is the translation of the *Seventy* interpreters,[25] commonly so called, which prepared the way for our Saviour among the Gentiles by written preaching, as Saint *John Baptist* did among the *Jews* by vocal. For the *Grecians,* being desirous of learning, were not wont to suffer books of worth to lie moulding in kings' libraries, but had many of their servants, ready scribes, to copy them out, and so they were dispersed and made common. Again, the *Greek* tongue was well known and made familiar to most inhabitants in *Asia,* by reason of the conquest that there the *Grecians* had made, as also by the colonies, which thither they had sent. For the same causes also it was well understood in many places of *Europe,* yea, and of *Africa* too. Therefore the word of God being set forth in *Greek,* becometh hereby like a candle set upon a candlestick, which giveth light to all that are in the house, or like a proclamation sounded forth in the market-place, which most men presently take knowledge of; and therefore that language was fittest to contain the Scriptures, both for the first preachers of the Gospel to appeal unto for witness, and for the learners also of those times to make search and trial by. It is certain, that that translation was not so sound and so perfect, but that it needed in many places correction; and who had been so sufficient for this work as the Apostles or apostolic men? Yet it seemed good to the Holy Ghost and to them to take that which they found (the same being for the greatest part true and sufficient) rather than by making a new, in that new world and green age of the

Church, to expose themselves to many exceptions and cavilla-
tions[26] as though they made a translation to serve their own
turn, and therefore bearing witness to themselves, their witness
not to be regarded. This may be supposed to be some cause,
why the translation of the *Seventy* was allowed to pass for
current. Notwithstanding, though it was commended generally,
yet it did not fully content the learned, no, not of the *Jews*. For
not long after *Christ, Aquila* fell in hand with a new translation,
and after him *Theodotion,* and after him *Symmachus*: yea, there
was a fifth and a sixth edition, the authors whereof were not
known. These with the *Seventy* made up the *Hexapla,* and were
worthily and to great purpose compiled together by *Origen*.
Howbeit the edition of the *Seventy* went away with the credit,
and therefore not only was placed in the midst by *Origen* (for
the worth and excellency thereof above the rest, as *Epiphanius*
gathereth) [*Epiphan. de mensur, et ponderibus.*] but also was used
by the *Greek* fathers for the ground and foundation of their
commentaries. [*See S. August. 2. de doctrin, Christian. c. 15
Novell, diatax,* 146.] Yea, *Epiphanius* above-named doth
attribute so much unto it, that he holdeth the authors thereof
not only for interpreters, but also for prophets in some respect:
and *Justinian* the Emperor, enjoining the *Jews* his subjects to
use specially the translation of the *Seventy,* rendereth this
reason thereof, because they were, as it were, enlightened with
prophetical grace. [προφητικη ωσπερ χαριτο περιλ-
αμψαση αυτου.] Yet for all that, as the *Egyptians* are said of
the Prophet [Isa. 31:3] to be men and not God, and their
horses flesh and not spirit: so it is evident, (and Saint *Hierome*
[*S. Hieron. de optimo genere interpret.*] affirmeth as much) that
the *Seventy* were interpreters, they were not prophets; they did
many things well, as learned men; but yet as men they stum-
bled and fell, one while through oversight, another while
through ignorance, yea, sometimes they may be noted to add
to the original, and sometimes to take from it; which made the

Apostles to leave them many times, when they left the *Hebrew,* and to deliver the sense thereof according to the truth of the word, as the Spirit gave them utterance. This may suffice touching the Greek translations of the Old Testament.

TRANSLATION OUT OF HEBREW AND GREEK INTO LATIN

There were also within a few hundred years after CHRIST translations many into the Latin tongue: for this tongue also was very fit to convey the Law and the Gospel by, because in those times very many countries of the West, yea of the South, East, and North, spake or understood Latin, being made provinces to the *Romans.* But now the Latin translations were too many to be all good, for they were infinite *Latini Interpretes nullo modo numerari possunt,* saith *S. Augustine.*) [S. Augustin. de doctr. Christ, lib. 2. cap. 11.] Again, they were not out of the *Hebrew* fountain (we speak of the *Latin* translations of the Old Testament) but out of the *Greek* stream, therefore the *Greek* being not altogether clear, the *Latin* derived from it must needs be muddy. This moved *S. Hierome,* a most learned father, and the best linguist without controversy, of his age, or of any that went before him, to undertake the translating of the Old Testament, out of the very fountains themselves; which he performed with that evidence of great learning, judgement, industry, and faithfulness, that he hath for ever bound the Church unto him, in a debt of special remembrance and thankfulness.

THE TRANSLATING OF THE SCRIPTURE INTO THE VULGAR TONGUES

Now though the Church were thus furnished with *Greek* and *Latin* translations, even before the faith of CHRIST was generally embraced in the Empire: [S. Hieronym. Marcell, Zosim.] (for the learned know that even in *S. Hierome's* time the Consul of *Rome* and his wife were both Ethnicks,[27] and about the same time the greatest part of the Senate also) yet for all that the godly-learned were not content to have the Scriptures in the language which themselves understood, *Greek* and *Latin* (as the good lepers [2 King. 7:9] were not content to fare well themselves, but acquainted their neighbours with the store that God had sent, that they also might provide for themselves) but also for the behoof[28] and edifying of the unlearned which hungered and thirsted after righteousness, and had souls to be saved as well as they, they provided translations into the vulgar for their countrymen, insomuch that most nations under heaven did shortly after their conversion hear CHRIST speaking unto them in their mother tongue, not by the voice of their minister only, but also by the written word translated. If any doubt hereof, he may be satisfied by examples enough, if enough will serve the turn. First, *S. Hierome* [S. Hieron. præf. in 4. Evangel.] saith, *Multarum gentium linguis Scriptura ante translata, docet falsa esse quæ addita sunt*, etc., i.e. *The Scripture being translated before in the languages of many nations, doth shew that those things that were added* (by *Lucian* or *Hesychius*) *are false.* The same Hierome elsewhere [S. Hieron. Sophronio.] affirmeth that he, the time was, had set forth the translation of the *Seventy, suæ linguæ hominibus*, i.e. for his countrymen of *Dalmatia*. Which words not only *Erasmus* doth understand to purport, that *S. Hierome* translated the Scripture into the *Dalmatian* tongue, but also *Sixtus Senensis*, [Six. Sen. lib. 4. Alphon à Castro lib. 1. ca. 23.] and *Alphonsus à Castro*, (that we speak of no more) men not to be excepted against by them of *Rome*, do ingenuously confess as much. So *S. Chrysostome*, [S. Chrysost. in Johan. cap. 1. hom. 1.] that lived in *S. Hierome's* time, giveth evidence with him: *The doctrine of S. John* (saith he) *did not in such sort* (as the philosophers did) *vanish away: but the Syrians, Egyptians, Indians,*

Persians, Ethiopians, and infinite other nations, being barbarous people, translated it into their (mother) tongue, and have learned to be (true) philosophers, he meaneth Christians. To this may be added *Theodorit* [Theodor. 5. Therapeut.] as next unto him both for antiquity, and for learning. His words be these, *Every country that is under the sun is full of these words* (of the Apostles and Prophets) *and the Hebrew tongue* (he meaneth the Scriptures in the *Hebrew* tongue) *is turned not only into the language of the Grecians, but also of the Romans, and Egyptians, and Persians, and Indians, and Armenians, and Scythians, and Sautomatians, and briefly into all the languages that any nation useth.* So he. In like manner, [P. Diacon. li. 12. Isidor, in Chron. Goth. Sozom. li. 6. cap. 37.] *Ulpilas* is reported by *Paulus Diaconus* and *Isidor* (and before them by *Sozomen*) to have translated the Scriptures into the *Gothic* tongue: *John* Bishop of *Seville* by *Vasseus,* to have turned them into *Arabic* about the year of our Lord 717: [Vaseus in Chron. Hispan.] *Beda* by *Cistertiensis,* to have turned a great part of them into *Saxon: Efnard* by *Trithemius,* to have abridged the French Psalter, as *Beda* had done the *Hebrew,* about the year 800: King *Alured* by the said *Cistertiensis,* to have turned the Psalter into Saxon: [Polydor. Virg. 5 histor. Anglorum testatur idem de Aluredo nostro.] *Methodius* by *Aventinus* [Aventin. lib. 4.] (printed at *Ingolstad*) [B. Rhenan. rerum German. lib. 2.] to have turned the Scriptures into [Circa annum 900.] *Sclavonian: Valdo,* Bishop of *Frising,* by *Beatus Rhenanus,* to have caused about that time the Gospels to be translated into *Dutch* rhythm, yet extant in the library of *Corbinian: Valdus,* by divers, to have turned them himself, or to have gotten them turned, into *French* about the year 1160: *Charles,* the fifth of that name, surnamed *The wise,* to have caused them to be turned into *French,* about 200 years after *Valdus's* time, of which translation there be many copies yet extant, as witnesseth *Beroaldus.* [Beroald.] Much about that time, even in our King *Richard* the Second's days, *John Trevisa* translated them into *English,* and many *English*

Bibles in written hand are yet to be seen with divers, translated, as it is very probable, in that age. So the *Syrian* translation of the New Testament is in most learned men's libraries, of *Widminstadius's* setting forth; and the Psalter in *Arabic* is with many, of *Augustinus Nebiensis's* setting forth. So *Postel* affirmeth, that in his travel he saw the Gospels in the *Ethiopian* tongue; and *Ambrose Thesius* allegeth the Psalter of the *Indians,* which he testifieth to have been set forth by *Potken* in *Syrian* characters. So that to have the Scriptures in the mother tongue is not a quaint conceit lately taken up, either by the Lord *Cromwell* in *England,* or by the Lord *Radevil* [Thuan.] in *Polonie,* or by the Lord *Ungnadius* in the Emperor's dominion, but hath been thought upon, and put in practice of old, even from the first times of the conversion of any nation; no doubt because it was esteemed most profitable to cause faith to grow in men's hearts the sooner, and to make them to be able to say with the words of the Psalm, *As we have heard, so we have seen.* [Ps. 48:8]

THE UNWILLINGNESS OF OUR CHIEF ADVERSARIES, THAT THE SCRIPTURES SHOULD BE DIVULGED IN THE MOTHER TONGUE, ETC.

Now the Church of Rome would seem at the length to bear a motherly affection towards her children, and to allow them the Scriptures in their mother tongue: but indeed it is a gift, not deserving to be called a gift, an unprofitable gift: [δωρον αδωρον κουκ ονησιμον. Sophocles.] they must first get a licence in writing before they may use them, and to get that, they must approve themselves to their confessor, that is, to be such as are, if not frozen in the dregs, yet soured with the leaven of their superstition. Howbeit, it seemed too much to *Clement* the Eighth that there should be any licence granted to have them in the vulgar tongue, and therefore he overruleth and frustrateth the grant of *Pius* the Fourth. [See the observation (set forth by Clement's authority) upon the 4th rule of Pius the IV's making in the Index, lib. prohib. pag. 15. ver. 5.] So much are they afraid of the light of Scripture, (*Lucifugæ Scripturarum,* as *Tertullian* speaketh) [Tertul. de resur. carnis.] that they will not trust the people with it, no not as it is set forth by their own sworn men, no not with the licence of their own bishops and inquisitors. Yea, so unwilling they are to communicate the Scriptures to the people's understanding in any sort, that they are not ashamed to confess that we forced them to translate it into *English* against their wills. This seemeth to argue a bad cause, or a bad conscience, or both. Sure we are, that it is not he that hath good gold that is afraid to bring it to the touchstone, but he that hath the counterfeit; neither is it the true man that shunneth [John 3:20] the light, but the malefactor, lest his deed should be reproved: neither is it the plain dealing merchant that is unwilling to have the weights or the meteyard brought in place, but he that useth deceit. But we will let them alone for this fault, and return to translation.

THE SPEECHES AND REASONS, BOTH OF OUR BRETHREN AND OF OUR ADVERSARIES, AGAINST THIS WORK

Many men's mouths have been open a good while (and yet are not stopped) with speeches about the translation so long in hand, or rather perusals of translations made before: and ask what may be the reason, what the necessity of the employment. Hath the Church been deceived, say they, all this while? Hath her sweet bread been mingled with leaven, her silver with dross, her wine with water, her milk with lime? (*Lacte gypsum malè misceture,* saith *S. Ireney.*) [S. Iren. 3. lib. cap. 19.] We hoped that we had been in the right way, that we had had the oracles of God delivered unto us, and that though all the world had cause to be offended and to complain, yet that we had none. Hath the nurse holden out the breast, and nothing but wind in it? Hath the bread been delivered by the fathers of the Church, and the same proved to be *lapidosus*, as *Seneca* speaketh? What is it to handle the word of God deceitfully, if this be not? Thus certain brethren. Also the adversaries of *Judah* and *Jerusalem*, like *Sanballat* in *Nehemiah*, mock, as we hear, both at the work and the workmen, saying: *What do these weak Jews, etc.? will they make the stones whole again out of the heaps of dust which are burnt? although they build, yet if a fox go up, he shall even break down their stony wall.* [Neh. 4:3] Was their translation good before? Why do they now mend it? Was it not good? Why then was it obtruded to[29] the people? Yea, why did the Catholics (meaning Popish *Romanists*) always go in jeopardy, for refusing to go to hear it? Nay, if it must be translated into English, Catholics are fittest to do it. They have learning, and they know when a thing is well, they can *manum de tabulâ*. We will answer them both briefly: and the former, being brethren, thus, with *S. Hierome, Damnamus veteres?* [S. Hieron. Apolog. advers. Ruffin.] *Minimè, sed post priorum studia in domo Domini quod possumus laboramus.* That is, *Do we condemn the ancient? In no case: but after the endeavours of them that were before us, we take the best pains we can in the house of God.* As if he said, Being provoked by the example of the learned that lived before my time, I have thought it my duty, to assay whether my talent in the knowledge of the tongues may be profitable in any measure to God's Church, lest I should seem to have laboured in them in vain, and lest I should be thought to glory in men (although ancient) above that which was in them. Thus *S. Hierome* may be thought to speak.

A SATISFACTION TO OUR BRETHREN

And to the same effect say we, that we are so far off from condemning any of their labours that travailed before us in this kind, either in this land or beyond sea, either in King *Henry's* time, or King *Edward's* (if there were any translation, or correction of a translation in his time) or Queen *Elizabeth's* of ever-renowned memory, that we acknowledge them to have been raised up of God, for the building and furnishing of his Church, and that they deserve to be had of us and of posterity in everlasting remembrance. The Judgement of *Aristotle* is worthy and well known: *If Timotheus had not been, we had not had much sweet music; but if Phrynis (Timotheus's* master) *had not been, we had not had Timotheus.* [Arist. 2. metaphys. cap. 1.] Therefore blessed be they, and most honoured be their name, that break the ice, and give the onset upon that which helpeth forward to the saving of souls. Now what can be more available thereto than to deliver God's book unto God's people in a tongue which they understand? Since of a hidden treasure, and of a fountain that is sealed, there is no profit, as *Ptolemy Philadelph* wrote to the Rabbins or masters of the Jews,[30] as witnesseth *Epiphanius*: [S. Epiphan. loco antè citato.] and as *S. Augustine* saith: *A man had rather be with his dog than with a stranger* (whose tongue is strange unto him.) [S. Augustin. lib. 19. de civil. Dei. c. 7.] Yet for all that, as nothing is begun and perfected at the same time, and the later thoughts are thought to be the wiser: so, if we building upon their foundation that went before us, and being holpen[31] by their labours, do endeavour to make that better which they left so good, no man, we are sure, hath cause to mislike us; they, we persuade ourselves, if they were alive, would thank us. The vintage[32] of *Abiezer,*[33] that strake the stroke: yet the gleaning of grapes of *Ephraim* was not to be despised. See *Judges 8, verse 2. Joash* the king of *Israel* did not satisfy himself, till he had smitten the ground three times; [2. Kings 13:18,19] and yet he offended the Prophet for giving over then. *Aquila,* of whom we spake before, translated the Bible as carefully and as skilfully as he could; and yet he thought good to go over it again, and then it got the credit with the Jews, to be called κατα ακριβειαν, that is, accurately done, as Saint *Hierome* witnesseth. [S. Hieron. in Ezech. cap. 3.] How many books of profane learning have been gone over again and again, by the same translators, by others? Of one and the same book of *Aristotle's* Ethics, there are extant not so few as six or seven several translations. Now, if this cost may be bestowed upon the gourd, which affordeth us a little shade, and which to-day flourisheth but tomorrow is cut down, what may we bestow, nay, what ought we not to bestow, upon the vine, the fruit whereof maketh glad the conscience of man, and the stem whereof abideth for ever? And this is the Word of God, which we translate. *What is the chaff to the wheat, saith the Lord?* [Jerem. 23:28] *Tanti vitrcum, quanti verum margaritum* (saith *Tertullian,*) [Tertul. ad Martyr.] [*Si tanti vilissimum, vitreum, quanti pretiosissimum Margaritum: Hieron. ad Salvin.*] if a toy of glass be of that reckoning with us, how ought we to value the true pearl? Therefore let no man's eye be evil, because his Majesty's is good;[34] neither let any be grieved that we have a Prince that seeketh the increase of the spiritual wealth of Israel (let *Sanballats* and *Tobiahs* do so, which therefore do bear their just reproof) but let us rather bless God from the ground of our heart, for working this religious care in him to have the translations of the Bible maturely considered of and examined. For by this means it cometh to pass, that whatsoever is sound already (and all is sound for substance, in one or other of our editions, and the worst of ours far better than their authentic vulgar) the same will shine as gold more brightly, being rubbed and polished; also, if anything be halting, or superfluous, or not so agreeable to the original, the same may be corrected, and the truth set in place. And what can the King command to be done that will bring him more true honour than this? and wherein could they that have been set a work, approve their duty to the King, yea, their obedience to God, and love to his Saints, more, than by yielding their service, and all that is within them, for the furnishing of the work? But besides all this, they were the principal motives of it, and therefore ought least to quarrel it: for the very historical truth is, that upon the importunate petitions of the Puritans, at his Majesty's coming to this crown, the conference at Hampton Court having been appointed for hearing their complaints, when by force of reason they were put from all other grounds, they had recourse at the last to this shift, that they could not with good conscience subscribe to the Communion book, since it maintained the Bible as it was there translated, which was, as they said, a most corrupted translation. And although this was judged to be but a very poor and empty shift, yet even hereupon did his Majesty begin to bethink himself of the good that might ensue by a new translation, and presently after gave order for this translation which is now presented unto thee. Thus much to satisfy our scrupulous brethren.

AN ANSWER TO THE IMPUTATIONS OF OUR ADVERSARIES

Now to the latter we answer, that we do not deny, nay, we affirm and avow, that the very meanest translation of the Bible in English, set forth by men of our profession, (for we have seen none of theirs of the whole Bible as yet) containeth the Word of God, nay, is the Word of God. As the King's Speech which he uttered in Parliament, being translated into *French, Dutch, Italian,* and *Latin,* is still the King's Speech, though it be not interpreted by every translator with the like grace, nor peradventure so fitly for phrase, nor so expressly for sense, everywhere. For it is confessed, that things are to take their denomination of the greater part; and a natural man could say, *Verùm ubi multa nitent in carmine, non ego paucis offendor maculis,* etc. [Horace.] A man may be counted a virtuous man though he have made many slips in his life, (else there were none virtuous, for *in many things we offend all* [James 3:2]) also a comely man and lovely, though he have some warts upon his hand, yea, not only freckles upon his face, but also scars. No cause therefore why the Word translated should be denied to be the Word, or forbidden to be current, notwithstanding that some imperfections and blemishes may be noted in the setting forth of it. For whatever was perfect under the sun, where Apostles or apostolic men, that is, men endued with an extraordinary measure of God's Spirit, and privileged with the privilege of infallibility, had not their hand? The Romanists therefore in refusing to hear, and daring to burn the Word translated, did no less than despise the Spirit of grace, from whom originally it proceeded, and whose sense and meaning, as well as man's weakness would enable, it did express. Judge by an example or two. *Plutarch* writeth, [Plutarch. in Camillo.] that after that *Rome* had been burnt by the *Gauls,* they fell soon to build it again: but doing it in haste, they did not cast the streets, nor proportion the house in such comely fashion as had been most sightly and convenient; was *Catiline* therefore an honest man, or a good patriot, that sought to bring it to a combustion? or *Nero* a good prince, that did indeed set it on fire? So, by the story of *Ezra* and the prophecy of *Haggai* it may be gathered that the Temple built by *Zerubbabel* after the return from *Babylon* was by no means to be compared to the former built by *Solomon* (for they that remembered the former wept [Ezra 3:12] when they considered the latter:) notwithstanding, might this latter either have been abhorred and forsaken by the *Jews,* or profaned by the *Greeks?* The like we are to think of translations. The translation of the *Seventy* dissenteth from the original in many places, neither doth it come near it for perspicuity, gravity, majesty; yet which of the Apostles did condemn it? Condemn it? Nay, they used it, (as it is apparent, and as Saint *Hierome* and the most learned men do confess) which they would not have done, nor by their example of using it, so grace and commend it to the Church, if it had been unworthy the appellation and name of the Word of God. And whereas they urge for their second defence of their vilifying and abusing of the *English* Bibles, or some pieces thereof, which they meet with, for that heretics, forsooth, were the authors of the translations, (heretics they call us by the same right that they call themselves Catholics, both being wrong) we marvel what divinity taught them so. We are sure *Tertullian* [Tertul. de præscript. contra hæreses.] was of another mind: *Ex personis probamus fidem, an ex fide personas?* Do we try men's faith by their persons? we should try their persons by their faith. Also *S. Augustine* was of another mind: for he, lighting upon certain rules made by *Tychonius,* a *Donatist,* for the better understanding of the Word, was not ashamed to make use of them, yea, to insert them into his own book, with giving commendation to them so far forth as they were worthy to be commended, as is to be seen in *S. Augustine's* third book *De Doctrinâ Christianâ.* [S. August. 3. de doct. Christ. cap. 30.] To be short, *Origen,* and the whole Church of God for certain hundred years, were of another mind: for they were so far from treading under foot, (much more from burning) the translation of *Aquila,* a proselyte, that is, one that had turned *Jew*; of *Symmachus,* and *Theodotion,* both *Ebionites,* that is, most vile heretics, that they joined them together with the *Hebrew* original, and the translation of the *Seventy* (as hath been before signified out of *Epiphanius*) and set them forth openly to be considered of and perused by all. But we weary the unlearned, who need not know so much, and trouble the learned, who know it already.

Yet before we end, we must answer a third cavil[35] and objection of theirs against us, for altering and amending our translations so oft; wherein truly they deal hardly, and strangely with us. For to whom ever was it imputed for a fault (by such as were wise) to go over that which he had done, and to amend it where he saw cause? Saint *Augustine* [S. Aug. Epist. 9.] was not afraid to exhort *S. Hierome* to a *Palinodia* or recantation; the same *S. Augustine* [S. Aug. lib. Retractat. *Video interdum vitia mea. S.*

Aug. Epist. 8.] was not ashamed to retractate, we might say revoke, many things that had passed him, and doth even glory that he seeth his infirmities. If we will be sons of the Truth we must consider that it speaketh, and trample upon our own credit, yea, and upon other men's too, if either be any way a hindrance to it. This to the cause. Then to the persons we say, that of all men they ought to be most silent in this case. For what varieties have they, and what alterations have they made, not only of their service books, portesses, and breviaries, but also of their *Latin* translation? The service book[36] supposed to be made by *S. Ambrose* (*Officium Ambrosianum*) was a great while in special use and request: but Pope *Adrian,* calling a Council with the aid of *Charles* the Emperor, abolished it, yea, burnt it, and commanded the service book of Saint *Gregory* universally to be used. [Durand. lib. 5. cap. 2.] Well, *Officium Gregorianum* gets by this means to be in credit, but doth it continue without change or altering? No, the very *Roman* service was of two fashions, the new fashion and the old, (the one used in one Church, the other in another) as is to be seen in *Pamelius,* a Romanist, his preface, before *Micrologus.* The same *Pamelius* reporteth out of *Radulphus de Rivo,* that about the year of our Lord 1277 Pope *Nicolas* the Third removed out of the churches of *Rome* the more ancient books (of service) and brought into use the missals of the Friars Minorites, and commanded them to be observed there; insomuch that about a hundred years after, when the above-named *Radulphus* happened to be at *Rome,* he found all the books to be new, (of the new stamp.) Neither was there this chopping and changing in the more ancient times only, but also of late: *Pius Quintus* himself confesseth, that every bishopric almost had a peculiar kind of service, most unlike to that which others had: which moved him to abolish all other breviaries, though never so ancient, and privileged and published by bishops in their dioceses, and to establish and ratify that only which was of his own setting forth, in the year 1568. Now, when the father of their Church, who gladly would heal the sore of the daughter of his people softly and slightly, and make the best of it, findeth so great fault with them for their odds and jarring, we hope the children have no great cause to vaunt of their uniformity. But the difference that appeareth between our translations, and our often correcting of them, is the thing that we are specially charged with; let us see therefore whether they themselves be without fault this way, (if it be to be counted a fault, to correct) and whether they be fit men to throw stones at us: *O tandem maior parcas insane minori*; [Horat.] they that are less sound themselves ought not to object infirmities to others. If we should tell them that *Valla, Stapulensis, Erasmus,* and *Vives* found fault with their vulgar translation, and consequently wished the same to be mended, or a new one to be made, they would answer peradventure, that we produced their enemies for witnesses against them; albeit they were in no other sort enemies than as *S. Paul* was to the *Galatians,* [Galat. 4:16] for telling them the truth: and it were to be wished that they had dared to tell it them plainlier and oftener. But what will they say to this, that Pope *Leo* the Tenth allowed *Erasmus's* translation of the New Testament, so much different from the vulgar, [Sixtus Senens.] by his apostolic letter and bull? that the same *Leo* exhorted *Pagnine* to translate the whole Bible, and bare whatsoever charges was necessary for the work? Surely, as the Apostle reasoneth to the *Hebrews,* [Heb. 7:11; 8:7] that *if the former Law and Testament had been sufficient, there had been no need of the latter:* so we may say, that if the old vulgar had been at all points allowable, to small purpose had labour and charges been under-gone about framing of a new. If they say, it was one Pope's private opinion, and that he consulted only himself; then we are able to go further with them, and to aver, that more of their chief men of all sorts, even their own *Trent*[37] champions, *Paiva* and *Vega,* and their own inquisitors, *Hieronymus ab Oleastro,* and their own bishop *Isodorus Clarius,* and their own cardinal

Thomas à Vio Caietan, do either make new translations themselves, or follow new ones of other men's making, or note the
vulgar interpreter for halting, none of them fear to dissent from
him, nor yet to except against him. And call they this an
uniform tenor of text and judgement about the text, so many of
their worthies disclaiming the now received conceit? Nay, we
will yet come nearer the quick: doth not their *Paris* edition
differ from the *Lovaine,* and *Hentenius's* from them both, and yet
all of them allowed by authority? Nay, doth not *Sixtus Quintus*
[Sixtus V. præfat. fixa Bibliis.] confess that certain Catholics (he
meaneth certain of his own side) were in such a humour of
translating the Scriptures into *Latin,* that Satan taking occasion
by them, though they thought of no such matter, did strive what
he could, out of so uncertain and manifold a variety of translations, so to mingle all things, that nothing might seem to be left
certain and firm in them, etc.? Nay, further, did not the same
Sixtus ordain by an inviolable decree, and that with the counsel
and consent of his cardinals, that the *Latin* edition of the Old
and New Testament, which the Council of *Trent* would have to
be authentic, is the same without controversy which he then set
forth, being diligently corrected and printed in the printing-
house of *Vatican?* Thus *Sixtus* in his preface before his Bible.
And yet *Clement* the Eighth his immediate successor, publisheth
another edition of the Bible, containing in it infinite differences
from that of *Sixtus* (and many of them weighty and material)
and yet this must be authentic by all means. What is to have the
faith of our glorious Lord JESUS CHRIST, with Yea and Nay, if
this be not? Again, what is sweet harmony and consent, if this
be? Therefore, as *Demaratus* of *Corinth* advised a great king,
before he talked of the dissensions among the *Grecians,* to
compose his domestic broils, (for at that time his queen and his
son and heir were at deadly feud with him) so all the while that
our adversaries do make so many and so various editions themselves, and do jar so much about the worth and authority of

them, they can with no show of equity challenge us for changing and correcting.

THE PURPOSE OF THE TRANSLATORS, WITH THEIR NUMBER, FURNITURE, CARE, ETC.

But it is high time to leave them, and to shew in brief what we proposed to ourselves, and what course we held, in this our perusal and survey of the Bible. Truly, good Christian reader, we never thought from the beginning that we should need to make a new translation, nor yet to make of a bad one a good one, (for then the imputation of *Sixtus* had been true in some sort, that our people had been fed with gall of dragons instead of wine, with whey instead of milk:) but to make a good one better, or out of many good ones, one principal good one, not justly to be excepted against; that hath been our endeavour, that our mark. To that purpose there were many chosen that were greater in other men's eyes than in their own, and that sought the truth rather than their own praise. Again, they came, or were thought to come, to the work, not *exercendi causâ* (as one saith), but *exercitati,* that is, learned, not to learn: for the chief overseer and εργοδιωκτη under his Majesty, to whom not only we, but also our whole Church was much bound, knew by his wisdom which thing also *Nasianzen* [Nazianzen. eiV rn. episk. parout. *Idem in Apologet.*] taught so long ago, that it is a preposterous order to teach first and to learn after, yea, that to εν πιθω κεραμειαν μανθανειν, to learn and practise together, is neither commendable for the workman, nor safe for the work. Therefore such were thought upon, as could say modestly with Saint *Hierome, Et Hebræum Sermonem exparte didicimus, et in Latino Penè ab ipsis incunabulis, etc. detriti sumus. Both we have learned the Hebrew tongue in part, and in the Latin we have been exercised almost from our very cradle. S. Hierome* maketh no mention of the *Greek* tongue, wherein yet he did excel, because he translated not the Old Testament out of *Greek,* but out of *Hebrew.* And in what sort did these assemble? In the trust of their own knowledge, or of their sharpness of wit, or deepness of judgement, as it were in an arm of flesh? At no hand. They trusted in him that hath the key of *David,* opening, and no man shutting;[38] they prayed to the Lord, the Father of our Lord, to the effect that *S. Augustine* [S. Aug lib. 11. Confess. cap. 2.] did: *O let thy Scriptures be my pure delight, let me not be deceived in them, neither let me deceive by them.* In this confidence and with this devotion, did they assemble together; not too many, lest one should trouble another; and yet many, lest many things haply might escape them. If you ask what they had before them, truly it was the *Hebrew* text of the Old Testament, the *Greek* of the New. These are the two golden pipes, or rather conduits, wherethrough the olive branches empty themselves into the gold.[39] Saint *Augustine* [S. August. 3. de doct. c. 3. etc.] calleth them precedent, or original, tongues; Saint *Hierome,* fountains. [S. Hieron. ad Suniam et Fretel.] The same Saint *Hierome* [S. Hieron. ad Lucinium, Dist. 9. ut veterum.] affirmeth, and *Gratian* hath not spared to put it into his decree, That *as the credit of the old books* (he meaneth of the Old Testament) *is to be tried by the Hebrew volumes, so of the New by the Greek tongue,* he meaneth by the original *Greek.* If truth be to be tried by these tongues, then whence should a translation be made, but out of them? These tongues, therefore, (the Scriptures, we say, in those tongues,) we set before us to translate, being the tongues wherein God was pleased to speak to his Church by his Prophets and Apostles. Neither did we run over the work with that posting haste that the *Septuagint* did; if that be true which is reported of them that they finished it in 72 days; [Joseph. Antiq. lib. 12.] neither were we barred or hindered from going over it again, having once done it, like *S. Hierome* [S. Hieron. ad Pammac. pro libr. advers. Jovinian.] if that be true which himself reporteth, that he could no sooner write anything, but presently it was caught from him, and published, and he could not have leave to mend it: neither, to be short, were we the first that fell in hand with translating the Scripture into English, and consequently destitute of former helps, as it is written of *Origen,* that he was the first, [πρωτοπειροι] in a manner, that put his hand to write commentaries upon the Scriptures, and therefore no marvel if he overshot himself many times. None of these things: the work hath not been huddled up in 72 days, but hath cost the workmen, as light as it seemeth, the pains of twice seven times seventy-two days, and more: [φιλει γαρ οκνειν πραγμ ανηρ πρασσων μεγα. *Sophoc. in Elect.*] matters of such weight and consequence are to be speeded with maturity; for in a business of moment a man feareth not the blame of convenient slackness. Neither did we think much to consult the translators or commentators, *Chaldee, Hebrew, Syrian, Greek,* or *Latin,* no, nor the *Spanish, French, Italian,* or *Dutch*; neither did we disdain to revise that which we had done, and to bring back to the anvil that which we had hammered: but having and using as great helps as were needful, and fearing no reproach for slowness, nor coveting praise for expedition, we have at the length, through the good hand of the Lord upon us, brought the work to that pass that you see.

REASONS MOVING US TO SET DIVERSITY OF SENSES IN THE MARGIN, WHERE THERE IS GREAT PROBABILITY FOR EACH

Some peradventure would have no variety of senses to be set in the margin, lest the authority of the Scriptures for deciding of controversies by that show of uncertainty should somewhat be shaken. But we hold their judgement not to be so sound in this point. For though *whatsoever things are necessary are manifest,* as *S. Chrysostome* saith, [παντα τα αναγκαια δηλα. S. Chrysost. in 2. Thess. cap. 2.] and as *S. Augustine, in those things that are plainly set down in the Scriptures, all such matters are found that concern Faith, Hope, and Charity*; [S. Aug. 2. de doctr. Christ. cap. 9.] yet for all that it cannot be dissembled,[40] that partly to exercise and whet our wits, partly to wean the curious from loathing of them for their everywhere plainness, partly also to stir up our devotion to crave the assistance of God's Spirit by prayer, and lastly, that we might be forward to seek aid of our brethren by conference, and never scorn those that be not in all respects so complete as they should be, being to seek in many things ourselves, it hath pleased God in His divine providence here and there to scatter words and sentences of that difficulty and doubtfulness, not in doctrinal points that concern salvation, (for in such it hath been vouched that the Scriptures are plain) but in matters of less moment, that fearfulness would better beseem[41] us than confidence, and if we will resolve, to revolve upon modesty with *S. Augustine,* (though not in this same case altogether, yet upon the same ground) *Melius est dubitare de occultis, quàm litigare de incertis*: [S. August. li. 8. de Genes. ad liter. cap. 5.] it is better to make doubt of those things which are secret, than to strive about those things that are uncertain. There be many words in the Scriptures [απαξ λεγομενα.][42] which be never found there but once, (having neither brother nor neighbour, as the *Hebrews* speak) so that we cannot be holpen[43] by conference of places.[44] Again, there be many rare names of certain birds, beasts, and precious stones, etc., concerning which the *Hebrews*[45] themselves are so divided among themselves for judgement, that they may seem to have defined this or that, rather because they would say something, than because they were sure of that which they said, as *S. Hierome* somewhere saith of the *Septuagint.* Now in such a case, doth not a margin do well to admonish the reader to seek further, and not to conclude or dogmatize upon this or that peremptorily? For as it is a fault of incredulity, to doubt of those things that are evident, so to determine of such things as the Spirit of God hath left (even in the judgement of the judicious) questionable, can be no less than presumption. Therefore as *S. Augustine* saith, [S.Aug. 2. de doctr. Christian. cap. 14.] that variety of translations is profitable for the finding out of the sense of the Scriptures: so diversity of signification and sense in the margin, where the text is not so clear, must needs do good, yea, is necessary, as we are persuaded. We know that *Sixtus Quintus* [Sixtus V. præf. Bibliæ.] expressly forbiddeth that any variety of readings of their vulgar edition should be put in the margin, (which though it be not altogether the same thing to that we have in hand, yet it looketh that way) but we think he hath not all of his own side his favourers for this conceit. They that are wise, had rather have their judgments at liberty in differences of readings, than to be captivated to one, when it may be the other. If they were sure that their high priest had all laws shut up in his breast, as *Paul* the Second bragged, [Plat. in *Paulo secundo.*] and that he were as free from error by special privilege as the dictators of *Rome* were made by law inviolable, it were another matter; then his word were an oracle, his opinion a decision. But the eyes of the world are now open, God be thanked, and have been a great while: [ομοιοπαθη. τρωτογ οι χρω εστι.] they find that he is subject to the same affections and infirmities that others be, that his skin is penetrable; and therefore so much as he proveth, not as much as he claimeth, they grant and embrace.

REASONS INDUCING US NOT TO STAND CURIOUSLY UPON AN IDENTITY OF PHRASING

Another thing we think good to admonish thee of, gentle reader, that we have not tied ourselves to an uniformity of phrasing, or to an identity of words, as some peradventure would wish that we had done, because they observe that some learned men somewhere have been as exact as they could that way. Truly, that we might not vary from the sense of that which we had translated before, if the word signified the same thing in both places [polushma.] (for there be some words that be not of the same sense everywhere) we were especially careful, and made a conscience, according to our duty. But that we should express the same notion in the same particular word; as, for example, if we translate the *Hebrew* or *Greek* word once by *purpose,* never to call it *intent*; if one where *journeying,* never *travelling*; if one where *think,* never *suppose*; if one where *pain,* never *ache*; if one where *joy,* never *gladness,* etc.; thus to mince the matter, we thought to savour more of curiosity than wisdom, and that rather it would breed scorn in the atheist than bring profit to the godly reader. For is the kingdom of God become words or syllables?[46] Why should we be in bondage to them, if we may be free? use one precisely when we may use another no less fit as commodiously? A godly father in the primitive time shewed himself greatly moved that one of newfangleness called κραβ-βατον σκιμπου, [A bed. Niceph. Calist. lib. 8. cap. 42.] though the difference be little or none; and another reporteth [S. Hieron. in 4. Jonæ. See S. Aug. epist. 10.] that he was much abused for turning *cucurbita* (to which reading the people had been used) into *hedera.*[47] Now if this happen in better times, and upon so small occasions, we might justly fear hard censure, if generally we should make verbal and unnecessary changings. We might also be charged (by scoffers) with some unequal dealing towards a great number of good English words. For as it is written of a certain great philosopher, that he should say, that those logs were happy that were made images to be worshipped; for their fellows, as good as they, lay for blocks behind the fire: so if we should say, as it were, unto certain words, Stand up higher, have a place in the Bible always, and to others of like quality, Get ye hence, be banished for ever, we might be taxed peradventure with *S. James's* words, namely, *To be partial in ourselves, and judges of evil thoughts.*[48] [λεπτολογια. αδολεσχια. το σπουδαζειν επι ονομασι. See Euseb. προπαρασκευη. li. 12. ex Platon.]

Add hereunto, that niceness in words was always counted the next step to trifling, and so was to be curious about names too: also that we cannot follow a better pattern for elocution than God himself; therefore He using divers words in His holy writ, and indifferently for one thing in nature, we, if we will not be superstitious, may use the same liberty in our English versions out of *Hebrew* and *Greek,* for that copy or store that he hath given us. Lastly, we have on the one side avoided the scrupulosity of the Puritans, who leave the old Ecclesiastical words, and betake them to other, as when they put *washing* for *Baptism,* and *Congregation* instead of *Church*: as also on the other side we have shunned the obscurity of the Papists,[49] in their *Azimes, Tunike, Rational, Holocausts, Præpuce, Pasche,* and a number of such like, whereof their late translation is full, and that of purpose to darken the sense, that since they must needs translate the Bible, yet by the language thereof it may be kept from being understood. But we desire that the Scripture may speak like itself, as in the language of Canaan, that it may be understood even of the very vulgar.

(CONCLUSION)

Many other things we might give thee warning of, gentle reader, if we had not exceeded the measure of a Preface already. It remaineth that we commend thee to God, and to the Spirit of His grace, which is able to build further than we can ask or think. He removeth the scales from our eyes,[50] the vail from our hearts,[51] opening our wits that we may understand His Word, enlarging our hearts, yea, correcting our affections, that we may love it above[52] gold and silver, yea, that we may love it to the end. Ye are brought unto fountains of living water which ye digged not; do not cast earth into them, with the Philistines, [Gen. 26:15] neither prefer broken pits before them, with the wicked Jews. [Jer. 2:13] Others have laboured, and you may enter into their labours.[53] O receive not so great things in vain; O despise not so great salvation![54] Be not like swine to tread under foot so precious things, [Matt. 8:34] neither yet like dogs to tear and abuse holy things. Say not to our Saviour with the *Gergesites*, Depart out of our coasts;[55] neither yet with *Esau* [Heb. 12:16] sell your birthright for a mess of pottage.[56] If light be come into the world, love not darkness more than light;[57] if food, if clothing, be offered, go not naked, starve not yourselves. Remember the advice of *Nazianzene,* [Nazianz. περι αγ. βαπτ. δεινον πανηγυριν παρελθειν και τηνικαυτα πραγματειαν επιζητειν.] *It is a grievous thing* (or dangerous) *to neglect a great fair, and to seek to make markets afterwards*: also the encouragement of S. *Chrysostome,* [S. Chrysost. in epist. ad Rom. Cap. 14. orat. 26. ιν ηθικ. αμηχανον σφοδρα αμηχανον.] *It is altogether impossible, that he that is sober (and watchful) should at any time be neglected.* Lastly, the admonition and menacing of S. *Augustine,* [S. August. ad artic. sibi falso object. Artic. 16.] *They that despise God's will inviting them, shall feel God's will taking vengeance of them.* It is a fearful thing to fall into the hands of the living God; [Heb. 10:31] but a blessed thing it is, and will bring us to everlasting blessedness in the end, when God speaketh unto us, to hearken; when He setteth His Word[58] before us, to read it; when He stretcheth out His hand and calleth, to answer, Here am I;[59] here we are to do thy will, O God.[60] The Lord work a care and conscience in us to know Him and serve Him, that we may be acknowledged of Him at the appearing of our Lord JESUS CHRIST, to whom with the Holy Ghost, be all praise and thanksgiving. Amen.

NOTES

1 Slandered, falsely accused.

2 Dislike, envy.

3 False argument.

4 History.

5 Discussion, from French *parler,* "speak."

6 I.e., Gaius Julius Caesar, of whom Plutarch wrote.

7 Reckoning, calculation.

8 Reproach, criticism.

9 I.e., Christian.

10 The term *chivalry* is related to *cavalry* and derives from French *cheval,* "horse." The meaning evolved because horse-riding knights were required to follow a code of conduct.

11 Abridger.

12 Evil, wickedness.

13 *S.* is an abbreviation for the title "Saint."

14 Jerome.

15 2 Corinthians 6:7; Ephesians 6:11–17.

16 Revelation 22:2.

17 Pantry, deriving from French *pain,* "bread."

18 Moldy.

19 Complete text.

20 Indicter, i.e., accuser.

21 Endowed.

22 2 Peter 1:4.

23 The Greeks used the term *barbarian* to denote someone who did not speak Greek.

24 The allusion is to the veil that separated the Holy Place from the Holy of Holies in the Israelite tabernacle and temple.

25 I.e., the Septuagint.

26 Frivolous objections.

27 Pagans.

28 Benefit.

29 Required, forced upon; cf. *intrude*.
30 Jewish tradition holds that Ptolemy Philadelphus, king of Egypt, employed seventy Jewish rabbis to translate the Old Testament into Greek, producing the Septuagint.
31 Helped.
32 Viticulture, growing of grapes.
33 Judges 8:2.
34 Cf. Matthew 20:15.
35 False argument.
36 Formal liturgy.
37 Alluding to the Council of Trent, called by the Catholic Pope to counter the Reformation then in progress, including a condemnation of popular translations and a reaffirmation of the authority of the Latin Vulgate.
38 Isaiah 22:22, said of Christ in Revelation 3:7.
39 Zechariah 4:2-3, 11–12.
40 Hidden, disguised.
41 Appear to, be suitable to.
42 The Greek term *hapax legomena* denotes rare terms (usually found in only one passage) in the Greek or Hebrew texts of the Bible whose meaning cannot be ascertained for certain because they are used in only one context.
43 Helped, assisted.
44 I.e., the word appears in but one place in the original text.
45 I.e., Jews.
46 1 Corinthians 4:20.
47 This alludes to something that happened in the time of Saints Jerome and Augustine. An earlier Latin version of Jonah 4:6–10 translated the Hebrew word *qiqayon* as *cucurbita,* "gourd." After consultation with Jewish rabbis, Jerome decided to render it *hedera,* "ivy," in his new Latin translation, the Vulgate. In A.D. 403, Augustine wrote Jerome that when his new translation of the Jonah passage had been read at Sunday services in Hippo, North Africa (where Augustine

was bishop), a riot ensued.

48 James 2:4.

49 Followers of the Pope, i.e., Roman Catholics.

50 Acts 9:18.

51 2 Corinthians 3:15.

52 More than.

53 John 4:38.

54 Cf. Hebrews 2:3.

55 Matthew 8:28–34.

56 Genesis 25:29–34.

57 John 3:19.

58 I.e., the Bible.

59 This is the usual response of ancient prophets when God spoke to them (Genesis 22:1, 11; 31:11; 46:2; Exodus 3:4; 1 Samuel 3:4; Isaiah 6:8; Acts 9:10).

60 Cf. Numbers 32:31; Psalms 40:8; 143:10; Hebrews 10:7, 9.

Index

Henry VI 9
Henry VII 9
Henry VIII 9, 11, 16, 20
Henry's Bible 12
Heptateuch 6
Hereford, Nicholas 7, 20
Holister, D. S. 43
Hollander, H. W. 23–26, 33
Hosea, Book of 46, 85

Isaiah, Book of 17, 19, 24, 25, 26, 39, 44, 45, 46, 48, 51, 52, 53, 55, 56, 57, 58, 59, 60, 61, 64, 65, 69, 70, 71, 72, 75, 82, 83, 84, 85, 86, 87, 88, 89, 90, 98, 102, 104, 128, 129
Israel 22, 52
Issachar, Testament of 25

Jacob, Book of 67
James 76
James I 1, 13, 16, 30, 91
James VI *See* James I
James, Book of 51, 54, 55, 58, 70, 72, 113, 129
Jarom, Book of 67
Jehovah 10 *See also* Jesus Christ
Jeremiah, Book of 24, 41, 44, 45, 47, 48, 51, 53, 54, 57, 59, 61, 62, 63, 65, 71, 72, 88, 89, 112, 125
Jeremiah, Epistle of 28
Jerome, Saint 5, 15, 19, 128
Jerusalem 6, 73, 80
Jesus Christ 27, 28, 31, 49, 59, 73, 76, 79, 80–81, 82, 88, 90, 128
Job 82, 84
Job, Book of 6, 26, 43, 44, 45, 46, 47, 48, 50, 51, 52, 53, 54, 55, 56, 57, 59, 60, 61, 62, 63, 64, 65, 67, 77
Joel, Book of 49, 54, 72
John 76
John the Baptist 27
John, Gospel of 6, 29, 31, 38, 39, 45, 46, 48, 49, 51, 52, 55, 56, 57, 58, 59, 61, 62, 64, 65, 66, 68, 70, 71, 72, 81, 83, 84, 87, 98, 102, 109, 129
Jonah, Book of 11, 39, 128
Joseph, Testament of 26
Joshua, Book of 6, 11, 32, 47, 50, 53, 56, 59, 62, 63, 65, 66, 71
Juda, Leo 13
Judah, Testament of 24
Jude, Book of 23, 31